# A Spoonful of Malt

A CIP catalogue record for this title is available from the British Library.

ISBN 9781788486088 (Paperback)
ISBN 9781788486095 (Hardback)
ISBN 9781788486101 (E-Book)

www.austinmacauley.com

First Published (2019)
Austin Macauley Publishers Ltd
25 Canada Square
Canary Wharf
London
E14 5LQ

Alan McCracken

# A SPOONFUL OF MALT

AUSTIN MACAULEY PUBLISHERS™
LONDON • CAMBRIDGE • NEW YORK • SHARJAH

This book is dedicated to my grandparents, William and Polly.

This gripping memoir of a boy growing up in the 1940s and '50s in the north of England tells of early years of warmth and happiness suddenly followed by coldness and mental abuse. His early life is spent with loving grandparents, but all changes when his father comes back from the war.

# Table of Contents

# My First Life

# A Little Boy

I was four years old. I was in a darkened parlour, standing by the side of a coffin. Without being told, I knew that the person lying in the coffin was my mother. Every time I went from the dining room to the stairs and passed the parlour, I had to tiptoe, and not speak or breathe loudly, which was a test, as my asthma made quiet breathing difficult at the best of times. After the coffin had gone, the parlour was forever out of bounds, unless I was accompanied by one of my grandparents. For a long time, I was not allowed to touch the closed curtains in my bedroom night or day, and in my grandmother's presence, I had to talk in whispers.

In this sad house, life went on, though gradually grief was subdued and life with these loving people, from that first memory until the last, some four years later, was the happiest time of my early life.

I sat countless times on the bottom step of the stairs looking out of the open front door, past the sweet-smelling, pinky-white climbing rose, down the unevenly flagged garden path to the permanently open gate, waiting eagerly for the first sight of my grandad trudging home from his work. He always looked old to me, nothing like the dark-haired handsome soldier, brave and smart, in the picture half-hidden in a shadowy alcove of the dining room. Now, alas, he seemed weary, though as soon as he spotted me eagerly waiting on that bottom stair, he always waved and smiled, and didn't look as tired.

When the last time was to arrive, Grandma told me to wave and smile as normal. He appeared in the distance, crossing our field, but by the time he reached the open gate, my eyes were brimming with tears. Though he was not one to show any emotion, his squeeze took all my breath away. But this was four years away.

Asthma brought "wheezing" days. Severe eczema brought "bleeding" days.

These times were like a stream losing its life, dying in its dry and dusty bed, or like fields parched white in the summer heat. On brighter days, when daredevil antics ended in tears and pain, then the stream was raging and frothing, the fields swampy, and the sky black, with a menacing, angry look that seemed to force me down into the very ground.

But every homeward step brought safety. Grandma's gentle voice and loving arms would ease all my pain and suffering. In her presence, the world was blue sky and warming sunshine, in green fields by clear and refreshing streams. She was a constant and steadying influence throughout those four happy years. Between the ages of four and eight years, my grandma and grandad were the cornerstones of my life.

I was a small, skinny, wheezing, camomile-covered lad, who often needed help. I turned to my heroes. Life became exciting, especially when Alan became Hopalong Cassidy, Johnny Mack Brown, Rockfist Rogan of the RAF, Wilson of the Wizard, Wally Hammond or Stanley Matthews. Sometimes Alan disappeared for the entire day. 'Well, lad, what have you been up to today?' was a question that could take some time to answer.

My brother Donald was a big boy who could always be relied on for protection. In unusual circumstances, our first instinct was to hold hands. On familiar territory, his name was extra ammunition – 'I'll tell my brother and he'll bash you up' – 'Give me that one and I'll tell my brother to pick you in his team.' "That one" could be a marble, a conker, a football, cricket or film star picture card, a milk bottle top, which we used to skim against the wall, or whatever was in vogue at the time.

Small, sweet and innocent, I thought of myself as clever, and able to achieve success through my superior intelligence. Grandad had his own ideas, and often brought me back to earth; as he often said, 'Eee, thar a rum lad'.

# Going the Distance

Rattling bones. My entire body rattled. Staring purposefully into the distance, I was facing my severest test. The reward? The life of a galley slave would be no match for failure.

Already some careful thought had gone into the preparation and build-up to this formidable journey. "Silence" had to be the operative word. A snake slithering and sliding, a panther with its stealth, or death in its stillness – all must be emulated in order to reach the objective unscathed. One pin-dropping sound would lead to disaster.

The journey was daunting. It was clear that if I crawled in a straight line towards the target, starting from a position of six o'clock and moved straight through to twelve o'clock, the path would remain an obstacle-free zone. The ability to read and pinpoint the enemy's exact position stemmed from expert sources, mainly Sergeant ACW Bourne, Rockfist Rogan's dependable navigator. This precise pinpointing, using the clock face method, was, apart from silence, my only ally, although I had gleaned a valuable insight into strategic planning procedures.

For instance, when you are facing danger of the highest order, then intelligence and common sense tell you not to expect weaknesses in the foe. No, it must be assumed he has none, and furthermore not only is he the enemy, he is the arch-enemy, with qualities bordering on perfection.

This particular enemy was situated on my left flank, entrenched in a fixed position. The time was fast approaching. Soon, there would be no turning back.

Throughout the ordeal, his giant shadow would be hovering menacingly across my path, a constant, looming threat.

It was 19:15 hours. The journey began. The enemy was instantly close by; I could hear his breathing, sometimes punctuated by silence as if through ears set to acute-detection mode, he was listening for any suspicious sounds. Despite all the intelligence that went into the planning of this operation, I had never realised the full impact of being in such close proximity. It was turning out to be a real test.

It was imperative to keep concentrating. Occasionally, strange rustling sounds, accompanied by some movement, would set my pulse racing. It was difficult to keep self-control, especially under that giant shadow.

Moving very slowly, I edged my way forward and reached the halfway position in safety. I couldn't recognise myself. "I" had become "it", and believe it or not, "it" didn't dare to breathe.

Elation rose. 'Don't count your chickens…' With victory imminent, the sound of the enemy's voice through the dark gloom dashed my hopes. In a soft and gentle voice, a strange and alien sound in the context, came the words, 'Goodnight, lad,' and then the command, 'Close the door behind you, and try and close it quietly.' It was 19:33 hours…

Later, we measured the room between the two doors; it was approximately six yards long; being eighteen feet, it worked out that, having taken eighteen minutes, I had been moving at one foot per minute.

The following evening, I was in my customary position on the bottom stair, watching for the first glimpse of Grandad coming home from work. He crossed the road into our field, through the open gate and up the long, uneven path. At the front door, he said those familiar but forever welcome words, 'Eee, thar a rum lad!' But on this occasion he ruffled my hair and gave me a penny, at the same time saying,

'Don't tell your Grandma.'

I had been a soldier, trying to crawl to safety past a dangerous enemy – Grandad, in his chair drowsing over the paper, and the distance to be covered was eighteen feet across the living room. He was not asleep, of course, but sitting quietly, hoping my grandma wouldn't appear and spoil things. He was also managing not to laugh, an achievement he later used as evidence of his strong self-discipline.

# One Day I Owned a Bicycle

It was the school holidays. The big day was close at hand, at last. I had waited for a long time.

But it was still not ready. The situation had to be faced. So, one evening…

'Will I ever get that bike, Grandma?'

'Of course you will, lad. Didn't your grandad tell you it would soon be ready?'

That's all he says, 'It's nearly fixed up.' But when I ask him how long will it be, he just says he has other jobs to do. In fact, he says he has a list, a mile long. What does he mean?'

'Hurry up and finish peeling them potatoes. If his tea's ready when he comes in, I'll ask him to get that bike fixed, so we can all have some peace.'

I worked on the potatoes and cabbage, peeling and cutting feverishly. Finally, everything was ready for Grandad's tea. He waved as he approached the open gate; I made a decision.

'Hello, Grandad.'

'Hello, Alan. Eee, it's good to be home, lad, to some peace and quiet.'

He was already making things difficult. Well, here goes.

'Grandad, Grandma's going to ask you to fix up my bike after tea. If it's not fixed up quick, it'll be too small for me.'

Well, I'd said it. Thankfully, Grandad wasn't angry. In fact, it looked as if he was trying not to laugh.

'Right, lad! There's not much to do. After my tea I'll just have a look at the paper and listen to the wireless, then I'll fix it up.'

Something had to be done. I knew if my grandad started reading his paper that would be it.

'While you're reading the paper, is it all right if I get the bike out of the shed, and all those bits and pieces, and put them in the backyard, Grandad, so when you come out they'll be all ready to fix?' My voice sounded strange and unconvincing.

'Listen, lad, if it starts raining you'd better put them all back in the shed.'

'It won't rain, Grandad.'

After tea, he was reading his paper. The wireless was switched on. Everything was peaceful. He was starting to fall asleep. I waited. Slowly he seemed to sink into the chair. The paper slipped from his hands, along with his promise to fix up my bike.

'Everything's ready, Grandad.'

His head lifted with a startled movement and he opened his eyes.

'OK, lad.' He began to rise from his chair. 'Eee, lad, your grandma's right. Until that bike's fixed up, we'll get no peace. Come on, then.'

That night sleep was difficult. Any plans for tomorrow were now abandoned.

I would be riding my bike. Grandad seemed very pleased to have finally fixed it up.

So the morning finally arrived. I was the proud owner of a two-wheeled bike. It wasn't new; in fact it was even older after my grandad had taken so long to fix it up. Most people would have turned up their noses if they had cast their eyes upon it, but for me, the day my grandparents gave me that bicycle can only be described as momentous.

The time taken in fixing up the bike had not been wasted. My friends' bikes had been useful allies in enabling the techniques of starting, pedalling, stopping and even cocking on and off to be mastered. Balancing, in front of the bikes' careful and scowling owners, had proven to be the most difficult. Anyway, on that day when that second or even seventh-hand two-wheeled bike was finally fixed up, I was ready.

Grandma's permission was needed before I could show off my treasure.

'Right, Alan, be careful, and keep off the busy roads.'

But such was my excitement my grandma's words seemed very far away. The moment I cocked on that two-wheeled bike, I was immediately transformed into my hero, the famous cowboy, Johnny Mack Brown.

In the distance were two Indians on horseback. 'Faster, faster!' My trusty steed responded willingly. Slowly, the distance narrowed. The thinking was simple – pass these two Indians, cut in front of them and force them into surrendering. The victorious Johnny Mack Brown then leads the captured Indians into town.

Passed their front and cutting across gave me a wonderful surge of exhilaration. Then one unforgettable moment brought disaster. My being of very tender age, still several years before double figures, and forgetting the rear wheel, resulted in this catastrophe. The back wheel of my bike, which unfortunately had not passed the two luckless Indians, became entangled with their front wheels, and we all fell sprawling into the road.

I heard language completely alien to me.

'*?%?*&?!' came this tirade amidst the mayhem.

This wasn't Apache; I had never heard words like this before. Finally one man said, in words I understood, 'You stupid daft fool! What do you think you're doing? You could have broken our necks! If I can get up I'll break yours!'

I didn't really know what had happened. One moment Johnny Mack Brown the hero; the next, just me, tangled up on the floor with my brain spinning as fast as my bicycle wheels.

'I'm sorry. My grandad's only just fixed up my bike, and it felt strange and wobbly.'

And then, without thinking, and without any immediate feelings of remorse, I told a lie.

'I've only just learned to ride a two-wheeler.'

'You shouldn't be on these roads then. You're a danger to the public, you stupid, daft boy – you could have killed us!' bawled the other man, who was clambering to his feet.

Then came a second lie.

'But it was my foot, it slipped off the pedal.'

The mention of the pedal set off worrying thoughts about the bike's condition, leading to tears. The men must have thought this was remorse, and the result was my receiving just a stern lecture and being told to go home. No harm had come to the bike and the lecture was soon forgotten, but the escapade did leave me wondering about those funny words.

The second incident was a mixture of daredevil stupidity and sheer bad luck. The "game" was to pedal fast towards a brick wall with your speed, decided by group agreement, being assessed at the point you stopped pedalling and started braking, with instant disqualification if you or the bike touched the wall. The one closest to the wall won. We all had several goes, and such was the competitive spirit within the group that greater and greater risks were taken.

My catastrophe occurred when, approaching the wall at breakneck speed, and standing high on the pedals, I felt the chain-link snap. I went sailing over the handlebars, head first into the brick wall, actually seeing stars, and had to be carried home.

Grandma was very upset.

'Oh, Alan, what's happened? Put him on the couch. Let me bathe that wound. I'll get some salt and water. I'll give you a big spoonful of malt and a drink of dandelion, and burdock.'

Treatment like this made me feel like it was worth hitting a brick wall. Malt was used as a medicine for children; Grandma used it also as a treat. I don't know what it was or what it was for, but it was sweet and sticky, made me feel better and most importantly, tasted good. And though the bruise above my left eye was sore, it made me look tough, like a returning war hero, especially when the soreness faded and the bruise started to darken.

That evening when Grandad arrived home from work, he saw me sitting as usual on the bottom stair.

'Hello, Grandad.'

'Hello, lad. Where have you been? On the Western Front?' He didn't seem over-concerned.

'No, Grandad. I hit a brick wall with my head when the chain-link snapped and I went head first over the handlebars. Will you mend my bike, Grandad?'

'If it's anything like you it'll be in a bad way,' came the consoling reply. It was consoling, in that, strangely, this reply made me feel even better than good.

The broken chain-link, being the only damage, was quickly repaired, so in the morning I could pedal again, but only after some persuasion.

'Grandma, please let me go on my bike. I promise I won't ride fast.'

'No, you'll end up being carried home again.'

It was in these situations that superior intelligence was required.

'But Grandma, if I don't go on my bike now, you'll still be worrying until I do, so I might as well go on it now, so you won't need to worry for all that time that I haven't been allowed to go on my bike.'

So it wasn't long before I was pedalling again.

My Grandma had succumbed to this superior reasoning, but still had the last word.

'Right, lad, listen carefully. Do not leave our field. Do you understand?'

'Yes, Grandma,' suddenly feeling both excited and impatient.

'Right. Well, off you go, and for goodness sake be careful!'

The front of the house was never classed as a road, street or avenue. It was just a fine, flattened, cindery dirt track running the entire length of the thirteen houses. The track in front of the houses varied in width from about ten to fifteen yards, and then simply faded unevenly into the field. So this advice, to stay in front of the house, I readily obeyed, happy just to ride my bicycle up and down the dirt track, from number thirteen down to number one and back again.

Then came the real disaster. The coalman's cart trundled up the track. I often wondered how one horse could pull such a heavy load. But it was a big horse. They always seemed to come up the middle of the dirt track, probably so the coalman could turn with the heavy sack on his back. He would come down to our house, heave a sack of coal on his back, and carry it all the way past number thirteen, around the side, and up the back of the houses. The number of times would vary, but it was always between ten and twenty times that he would trudge round the side of number thirteen. Watching him would leave me thinking that our coalman was one of the strongest men in the world.

On that pedalling day Grandma brought him out a drink; after he took off his thick leather back protector, I discovered that I could hardly even lift it.

'Hello, Alan,' said Mr Eccleston, drinking his tea. 'Where have you been? On the Western Front?'

'No, I hit a brick wall when I was riding my bike.'

'Did you cry?'

'No, but I saw stars.'

'What did your grandma say?'

'She gave me some malt and some dandelion and burdock.'

'Eee, you're a lucky lad. Well, I don't know about dandelion and burdock, but you can tell your grandma that tea was good. I suppose I'd better take a few bags of coal around the back. See you later, Alan.'

'OK, Mr Eccleston.'

He disappeared. At first, it was fun just to pedal past the horse and cart on one side and, turning at number thirteen, pass them on the other side and race, like Reg Harris, down to number one. This soon changed to pedalling round and round the stationary horse and cart. Then, because the horse was big, it seemed possible to be able to crouch down and ride underneath it like riding under a bridge.

I tried it. The bike seemed to collapse underneath the horse. All around me noise and chaotic movement, all made by the clattering horse. My eyes opened to find me lying under it, between its flailing legs, with hooves crashing and thudding into the ground around me.

'Come here, lad. Just sit there.' In one effortless movement I was safe, hauled to safety by the coalman.

'Whoa, boy, steady, steady. Good boy, Blackie, steady.' In soothing tones, he calmed the terrified horse.

Attracted by the commotion, several neighbours had already arrived at the scene. My grandma, looking flustered, was feeling my arms and legs.

'Alan, move your arm. Move the other one. Move your foot. Move the other one. Let me help you to stand up.'

Then, after these preliminary urgent checks, she said, 'Are you all right? How do you feel? Can you walk? Turn round! Let me have a good look at you. What happened? Did you slip on the dirt?'

I found it impossible to answer a question. She never seemed to take a breath, and all the time, she was checking my arms and legs. At last, she turned to the extremely concerned-looking audience and with a deep-sounding sense of relief told them, 'He's not hurt.'

'Thank you, Mr Eccleston, for pulling Alan clear of Blackie. I don't know how it happened. Will you take his bicycle and all the bits and pieces round the back, and put them in our backyard?' said Grandma, now looking more like her usual self.

My bike! Because of all the commotion, I had actually forgotten about it. Now the result of my reckless deed was apparent. The horse's hooves had smashed my treasure into a mangled mess.

'OK,' replied Mr Eccleston, 'but between you and me, this bike has had it. It's just about had its day. Just think how many miles that bike's done, and it's finished up under Blackie's feet.'

'Thanks, Mr Eccleston,' said Grandma, still grateful, but now slightly impatient.

'Alan, you go into the house now. See you next month, Mr Eccleston.'

Then, with two or three neighbours still staring at the bike, mumbling, 'That could have been Alan,' Grandma ushered me up the garden path.

Not being allowed out for the rest of that day didn't feel like a punishment; in fact, it wasn't intended to be one. The day was spent either reading or helping Grandma with her jobs. She occasionally would stop and stare at the bits and pieces piled up in the yard.

When it was near the time for Grandad to arrive home, she told me to go and wait in my bedroom. He came in and I heard them both quietly talking.

From the moment Mr Eccleston pulled me from under Blackie's feet until this moment, I hadn't been scolded in any way whatsoever. What was Grandad going to do? Never mind my narrow escape. Even if you reduced the "age" of fixing up my bicycle into hours, he had still put a lot of time and effort into fixing it up. In what way would he remind me of his hard labour? Words? Or actions?

'Right, Alan, your tea's ready.'

On opening the heavier than usual dining room door, I heard words that gave me reassurance.

'Here's a nice big tea, Alan,' Grandma said affectionately. 'You've had a really scary day.'

Grandad nodded wisely in agreement.

'Grandma's told me all about your accident, Alan. You've been a very lucky lad. Not like your bike. It's had it.'

I just agreed, and ate all my tea.

I have ridden lots of bicycles since then, but have never had one of my own. It was obvious even to me that I wouldn't be able to ask Grandad to fix up a bike again.

# A Day with the Americans

The day the Americans came to town, most of the street was in a state of intense anticipation of the unknown being revealed. People were talking – 'I wonder what they're like?' 'They'd better keep away from my daughter.' 'They shouldn't be here, they should be fighting, like my lad.' 'They'll probably turn up late again.' I stood on the pavement, quietly listening, beginning to wonder if we were fighting the Americans; nobody seemed to like them.

When the Americans finally trundled past, the watching people forgot their hostility and cheered loudly. The line of slow-moving vehicles seemed endless. I kept hearing people murmuring, 'Left-hand drive.' Even now, years later, I still think of the Americans driving with one hand – their left hand.

Shortly after this spectacular arrival, I wandered down the track which led out of our field. Crossing the road, still with tramlines, I entered another field, went down the track and into the park. It had never been as full. Large patches of the grass were densely covered with people, sitting or lying, enjoying the warm sunshine; it was impossible to walk in a straight line. The men were mostly Americans in uniform, and strangely each American had his arm around a woman. Walking, sitting or lying down, it was the same – an American and a woman.

Just inside the park entrance, an American and his girl were lying in the longer grass. I ignored them, and went further into the park, until I was surrounded by Americans. It would be easy now.

'Any gum, chum?'

The answers, though, were all of a similar nature – 'Get lost, kid' or 'Beat it.' Some just grinned. I soon became discouraged, not thinking that they too must have been fed up of hearing those three words.

My great expectations melting fast, I started up the slope towards the swings and roundabouts, and spotted two Americans without their arms around women.

'Any gum, chum?'

'Are you clever, kid?'

'Yes.'

'Can you count up to ten?' asked the second American.

'Course, it's easy.'

'Right, kid, turn 'round and count slowly to ten and it's yours,' the first American said, waving a stick of chewing gum.

'Listen, kid,' said the second American, 'Don't look back until you've counted slowly and loudly up to ten.'

After excitedly counting slowly and clearly from one to ten, I turned back round. My face dropped. No chewing gum, no Americans, just two figures slowing down at the bottom of the hill. One looked back. They must have thought they were at a safe distance.

It was disappointingly easy to follow them and keep out of sight, even when I had edged close. Not once did they look back to see if they were being followed. They wandered past the duck pond, through the ornamental gardens and out of the park at one of the side entrances. Nothing exciting happened. The streets, like the park, were full of people, so it wasn't hard to remain concealed. The Americans stopped at a house door. They both went in. What to do? I knocked on the door. A woman appeared.

'Hello. What do you want?' she asked, very pleasantly.

'Err, where's them Americans? I saw them just going in.' My voice sounded strange; the woman had surprised me.

Just then one of them appeared. It was the second American. He had unbuttoned his tunic with the flashing brass buttons, and looked more relaxed.

'I've counted up to ten. Can I have my gum, chum?'

A great guffaw and a bellow brought out the first American and another woman.

'Look at this, Buzz, that kid's here.'

The first American stared at me.

'Gee, it's kids like you that's winning this war,' he said. 'Hang on a minute, kid.'

The two women stood outside the door, smiling. The second American, standing in the doorway, was shaking his head in silent thought.

'What made you follow us, kid?'

'You promised me some chewing gum, and you were my last chance.'

'You did a swell job. We never spotted you.'

Just then the first American reappeared.

'Here you are, kid. You deserve it.'

I walked back to the park holding ten packets of chewing gum, whistling and no longer fed up.

Back at the park, the crowd of people reminded me of the time my grandad had taken me to a football match. But now everyone seemed to be coming towards me, pushing me back. I finally manoeuvred my way through the mass to where I could take three or four steps, then dodge, then seven or eight steps, dodge, then reach open grass at last.

It looked strange to see all the Americans going in the direction of town, when it was home time. Happily, I made my way towards my exit. Just before the park gate was the spot in the long grass, now vacant, where the American and his woman had been lying. I sauntered over. Staring up at me from the flattened grass was a medal, in the shape of a cross; connected to the medal was coloured ribbon. This was treasure indeed, but nothing compared to the knife that lay beside it. The blade and handle were longer than a twelve-inch ruler. It felt very sharp, and looked shiny. I wondered how many people had been killed by that blade, and what the American had done to win that medal.

Walking home, I struggled to work out how I could keep this knife without Grandma and Grandad finding out. Taking it straight into the house was too dangerous. In the end, it was easy. I hid the knife in one of my safe places in our field. Then, when the opportunity arose, with Grandad in his greenhouse and Grandma three doors down, talking to Mrs Whitaker, I sneaked the knife into my bedroom.

The hiding place was under the bed, in the middle of stored cardboard boxes which I had never seen disturbed. Quite regularly at first, then petering down to occasionally, I used to open the treasures and stare and wonder where they really came from. Had the American earned them for bravery, or had he stolen them from a dead enemy? Had he, on discovering his loss, blamed the woman for stealing his treasures.

I never told my grandparents, but when it came time for me to move away from them, to another life, I found they had disappeared, never to be seen again.

# The Headmaster

I often felt ill, suffering from asthma and eczema, yet apart from medical check-ups at the local hospital and a one-day truanting escapade, I cannot remember having any time off school. This excellent attendance record probably provided a stability that helped me to be good at school in both lessons and behaviour.

Reading comics was a further help. I was reading the older boys' comics at a very young age. My grandparents bought one for me every fortnight; having read it from the first page to the last, I would then swap it for a friend's comic, which in turn would be swapped for another friend's. This continuing exchange meant open access to a long list every month – picture comics such as Dandy, Beano, Film Fun and Radio Fun, and ones with stories, such as Rover, Adventure, Wizard, Hotspur and Champion. Reading probably gave me confidence, making school lessons seem easy.

Because of my good record, the headmaster, Mr Harris, would occasionally tap me on the head and say, 'Well done, Alan.' This made me feel good; praise from a headmaster is praise indeed.

He was very strict, but rarely shouted. For some reason, maybe simply because he was the headmaster, we were all frightened of him. When he was nearby, even the teacher's voice changed and the naughtiest children became well behaved.

At dinner time he patrolled up and down the aisles, and woe betide any child who was not eating in the correct manner. Having spotted a misdemeanour, perhaps two aisles distant, he would make his way there, and even though the culprit had changed to correct knife and fork mode, he would receive a hard rap on the knuckles. A girl offender would be told to stand up straight, then about five minutes later to sit down and eat properly.

Because it was a church school, Sunday School was held in the hall. My grandma insisted I went. It was war time, so maybe that was why most of the groups were looked after by the teachers from the day school, both infant and junior. The Sunday groups were quite small, with usually about ten children to each group.

Occasionally, the headmaster took charge of a group for a one-off religious lesson.

Once the subject was "Eternal Life" and how when people died they went to Heaven, but could see absolutely everything that we were doing on earth. Normally, these lessons were not very interesting, but that afternoon was quite different. I probably forced myself to listen because the teacher was the headmaster, but then gradually became interested in what he was saying. His words seemed very true to me. My mother could actually see what I was doing! Nobody had ever told me this before. I was so amazed by this revelation that I plucked up enough courage to ask the headmaster a direct question. Very few children had ever been so bold.

'Can my mother see me in school? Can she see me at home with my grandma? And outside, when I'm playing? Even what I'm thinking?' The questions tumbled out.

'She certainly can, Alan,' replied the Headmaster. 'She will be very pleased with you in your school work, and your grandma has told me you are a very good little boy. She tells me that you help her with all the jobs that need doing. She says she doesn't know what she'd do without you.'

I became silent. My thoughts were whizzing about eternal life and about my grandma, who had actually spoken to the Headmaster. Just as he finished answering my question, another strange thing happened. He told us to turn to a page in our Sunday School book and read quietly. The usual procedure was that we would read aloud individually.

In silent reading at the day school, we did not dare look up from our books. It was just the same at the Sunday School, especially with Mr Harris being the teacher. However, on this occasion I looked up. To my amazement, I was looking at the headmaster silently crying, wiping quickly the tears falling onto his face. He didn't see me looking, but at the end of that Sunday School lesson, he ruffled my hair with two hands, pressing quite firmly on the top of my head. At the same time he looked at me with a very thoughtful gaze. I had never been so close to the face of the headmaster. Close up, he looked old and tired, but also kind and gentle. It made me think of my grandad. Eventually, he silently pushed me on my way. I wondered why he never spoke, and why something in my mind warned me not to tell my friends that I had seen the headmaster crying.

Shortly after that Sunday, another incident occurred, this time on a weekday, at the end of school. We had Physical Training as our last lesson. Most of the class would go home without changing, but grandma disapproved of this, so on PT day, I would be one of the last to leave.

The changing room was our classroom; the door opened onto the hall. It was never decided who threw first, but this other lad and I were furiously waging war, throwing plimsolls at each other, when suddenly the classroom door opened. One of them hit the headmaster directly on the top of his head. The voice that bellowed, ‘My room!’ was unrecognisable, and filled me with terror. I was first. From the moment he pulled me into his room by the ear to the moment he pushed me out again, he said only four words, ‘Bend over – get out.’ In between those four words, I had six of the very best. I left crying, though always denied it.

# The Yellow Stuff

In those years, several years before double figures, I must have looked a pitiful sight: arms and legs and neck a mass of weeping, semi-dry, bleeding scurvy, all covered in white camomile lotion, clutching at whatever I could as an aid to breathe. Letting go of "whatever" would cause me to collapse into a heap.

Sometimes breathing was so difficult my eyes felt as if they were leaving their sockets. On these severe days, playing or running about having fun was impossible. But on better days football, cricket, sword fights, sprint races, play fighting, or whatever boyish activity was in mode at the time, would find me leaping about with all my friends.

On one of these wonderful fun days, I came running happily into the house, where I was met by Grandad's serious face.

'Alan, your grandma wants to speak to you.'

Whenever these words were spoken by either of them, there was usually something important about to happen. There was no time to think, only to feel alarmed. But I never expected this.

'Listen, Alan,' said Grandma quietly, 'for a little while, you won't be playing at football or cricket. I don't want you to be running or jumping about.'

'But Grandma, what do you mean? Why can I not run about? My asthma and eczema haven't stopped me before, unless they were really bad.'

'I'm sorry, Alan, but don't let me see you running and jumping and fighting.'

'Do you understand what your grandma is saying?' said Grandad.

'Yes, Grandad.' His voice also had sounded final.

'Right, well, listen carefully,' said Grandma, now sounding very serious. 'Starting from today, every night before you go to bed, I'll be giving you some new medicine. It will help to build you up and make you big and strong.'

'But Grandma, I am strong. I can nearly lift the coalman's leather protector, and that's really heavy. I don't want to be any stronger.'

My resistance was useless.

'Alan, you'll be having a glass of this medicine every night.'

She stored it in a great big jar on a very high shelf, and gave me a small glassful every night. It was yellow, and, unlike the doctor's bottled medicine, which tasted horrid, this tasted sweet. At first, it was just thick, but very quickly it developed lumps. I was drinking lumps of yellow stuff every night in an effort to build me up. This medicine became my pet hatred. When I swallowed a lump, my throat and stomach would rebel and do their best to reject it. It came down to sheer will power every dreadful night.

I didn't know at that time that the real reason for my not partaking in games and for taking the yellow medicine was because Grandma suspected some form of tuberculosis. She thought this medicine was very important as a means of building me up. But I hated it, and had to think of ways of escaping it, even if for just one night.

'Grandma, this medicine is all lumpy; it's making me sick.'

'Can I miss my medicine tonight? I can't breathe.'

'Can I take my medicine tomorrow morning before I go to school?'

'Can I have a smaller glass?'

'If you let me miss tonight, I'll have two glasses in the morning.'

But the answer was always the same.

'Alan, every night you'll have a glass of this medicine, whatever you say. Just take your time and sip it. Don't gulp it down, then you won't be sick.'

It became a torture to me, and it happened every night. It took me longer and longer to drink the medicine. It reached the point where my grandma had to leave me to it.

'Just remember, I want to see an empty glass when you say goodnight.'

Not long after Grandma "left me to it", a lump or two of the medicine managed to disappear down the sink. Anyway, the inevitable happened, and subsequent nights saw me pouring away the entire contents of the glass and swilling away the lumpy evidence. The perfect solution.

I don't really know how Grandma found out. The only blatant error was the timing; the process of taking my medicine had speeded up considerably. It must have created some suspicion. Whether she planned to catch me in the act or whether it was completely by accident, one night Grandma caught me pouring the entire glassful of yellow lumps into the sink. Then came the moment I will never forget.

She grabbed me by the scruff of the neck and slapped and slapped and slapped, continuously, in the kitchen, across the room, down the passage, up the stairs, and into the bedroom. The suspected TB was forgotten. The eczema on my arms and legs was irrelevant. My grandma was shouting throughout the entire ordeal; all I can remember was "coupons" and "eggs" and "scarce". The slappings increased as I reached the bed. Then suddenly they stopped and she disappeared from the room. It was never mentioned again, and the high shelf was empty from then on. A few days after my thrashing, Grandma called me over.

'Right, Alan, come and sit down near me. Now listen very carefully. Here is some medicine from the doctor. You have to take it three times a day. I will give you the medicine. It will probably taste horrid. Please do not complain. Do you understand, Alan?'

'Yes, Grandma.' I knew it would taste awful, but at least it wouldn't be lumpy.

'And listen carefully, Alan. Please do not be running and jumping about with your friends. I'll be very angry if you do'.

'All right, Grandma, I won't.'

The experience with the yellow stuff had made me unhappy. But I had never seen my grandma so angry, and that now was making me sad. She had never hit me like that before, and she would never hit me like that again. From that night, all my efforts went into keeping in her good books.

# Our Railway Book

In April, when I turned four, I was only three years younger than my brother, but by the time July came along I was four years younger than him, or, as he would always claim, he was four years older than me. It seemed I would never catch him up.

Donald towered head and shoulders over me, not because he was tall, but because I was small. He looked, and was, healthy, with a sturdy frame, compared to me, who looked like a waif, a skinny weakling. He had dark brown hair, and mine was fair, especially in summer when it turned nearly white. Except for that four year age gap these differences never bothered me. In fact, when people first remarked upon them Grandma's answer made me feel good.

'They don't look like brothers. Just look at them.' The stranger's voice was filled with incredulity. I was filled with alarm. What did people see when they looked at me?

'I mean, Alan looks so small and weak and –'

Suddenly, Grandma interrupted. 'Alan takes after his mother's side, so he'll be all right.' Her voice was calm and reassuring. I felt better.

In Donald's company, I always felt safe. Any time we left the comfortable boundaries of our playing area, he was told to look after me. Grandma did allow me some freedom. For a start, there was "our field". In our field were thirteen terraced cottages with long front and back gardens; we lived at number 12. My grandparents always referred to the field as "our field", and here I felt completely safe. On one side of our field lay one or two streets where most of our friends lived. On the other, under the railway bridge, was the fishing pond. Behind the row of cottages, via the railway track, were some areas of open land and a few conker trees. In front of our field was the road, with the tramlines; crossing the road you could enter the field that led into the park. In all these areas Donald didn't have to look after me – so he didn't. He played with children of his own age, or slightly older. Any time we went into town, or to visit relatives, he was in charge.

On one trip to town, I was going to fulfil a dream. Two shillings, saved over a long period of time, would enable me to buy a Railway Book. In this book would be a complete list of all the train numbers and names, listed in different classes, such as *Jubilee* or *Patriot*. All the way to town I was happy, but Donald looked miserable. At last, we reached the shop. I went in by myself, leaving Donald sulking. This didn't bother me, especially when the shopkeeper smilingly asked what I would like.

'A brand new Railway Book, please.'

'Well, lad, let me see if there are any left. Everybody has been asking for a Railway Book,' said the shopkeeper.

My heart nearly stopped. I hadn't thought that they would have sold out.

'Oh, here we are, lad. Wow, that pile of Railway Books has dwindled. There are only three left.'

'Please don't wrap it up.' I placed the two shillings on the counter.

'Right, lad, here's your Railway Book. I bet you're as old as me before you've spotted all them.'

I grasped the book eagerly, blurted out my thanks and left the shop.

The shop door hadn't time to close before Donald spoke. 'Let me have a look, Alan.'

I ignored him. It was an incredible feeling, opening the book. A book crammed with numbers and names. Which train would be underlined first? My head was spinning as each page was turned.

'Let's have a look at it, please, Alan.' Donald always said please when he wanted something badly.

'Here you are then. Do you wish you had one?'

He nodded dejectedly as he turned over the pages.

'Listen, Alan, if I promise to give you my silver threepenny bit every month for a whole year, will you let me have this Railway Book?' We both received a threepenny bit on our monthly visits to our other grandad.

'No.'

'But that means you'll have three shillings, and the Railway Book is only two shillings.'

'Give it back, or I'll tell Grandma.' She knew why we had gone into town. She knew I had been saving up for a long time. This threat was enough.

'Here.' Donald thrust the book into my hand.

He was fed up and angry, both at the same time. In these situations he walked quickly, forcing me to run to keep up. That day was a running day. My brother's longing for my Railway Book meant that I had to keep it hidden away from him.

One day, a group of us decided to go to the park for some chewing gum, the source of our supply being the Americans.

Because the railway track was in view from the park, I decided to take my Railway Book. We were doing the usual loitering when this menacing boy came along. Just looking at him scared me; he was massive. He spotted the book.

'Give me that book, kid.'

'No, get one of your own.' Feeling the comfort of my allies I sounded brave.

He lunged forward threateningly.

'Give me that book.'

I couldn't speak. My brother and the other boys looked scared. If he grabbed hold of me, I had no chance. Now my back was against the railway bank wall.

The bully, towering over me, took out a jackknife. He raised the open-bladed knife high above his head, and, with a sneering voice, threatened to throw it at me. 'You've got one last chance, you stupid kid. Give me that book.'

I stayed silent, clutching my book in two hands.

We had often played a game, using a stone. The usual procedure, with your hand above your head, ready to throw, was to let go of the stone so that it fell harmlessly behind your back. Even so, when a hand came at you in a throwing motion, it would always make you jump. But now it wasn't a game. This was a real bully, and this real bully didn't let go until his hand flailed forward. It was a good job that my reaction was to duck rather than jump. The jackknife hit the railway-banking stone wall just where my head had been. That's when Donald intervened.

'Pick on somebody your own size, you big bully!'

I looked up to see Donald, half the bully's size, rushing at him.

'You stupid kid – you've asked for it now!' The bully's attention, thankfully for me, turned on Donald.

In the ensuing fight, which my brother lost, he received what would end up as a very black eye. I say Donald lost the fight; that may not be quite correct. He was certainly on the receiving end of more punches. However, the fight stopped when he landed one good punch on the bully's face. Abruptly, the bully stepped back.

'Just you wait, you lot, you've had it. Especially you,' he scowled, looking at Donald, 'you stupid kid.'

He picked up his jackknife with another menacing scowl, and moved off, still voicing threats, but now his hand was rubbing what I hoped was a sore face.

We all turned towards Donald. He was the hero.

'Thanks, Donald, for sticking up for me. He frightened me.'

'That's all right, Alan. I was frightened too, especially when he threw that jackknife. Thank goodness he's gone.'

'It was when you punched his face. I hope you hurt him, Donald.'

'So do I. He hurt me,' said Donald, gingerly feeling his face.

At that we made our way, without loitering, into the park, where we fitted in our trainspotting at every warning shout of 'There's a train coming!' However, the main objective was chewing gum from the Americans. I realised that day that unpleasant things could be used to some advantage to the one suffering the unpleasantness.

My brother used his sore eye to the limit.

'Hey, kid, where did you get that eye?'

'Well, I had to fight this lad who was bullying my little brother and –'

'Gee, kid, you have a real shiner.'

'Well, I had to fight this lad who was bullying my little brother and –'

'Wow, kid, what about the other guy?'

'Well, I had to fight this lad who was bullying my little brother and –'

It is a fair estimate that Donald took at least four times as much chewing gum home as anybody else that day.

On our way home, just as the park narrowed towards the exit, we found ourselves in trouble, or, more exactly, Donald did. The bully and another lad of similar size were waiting in the undergrowth by the side of the grass. They didn't seem interested in my Railway Book. They went straight for Donald. Before he knew what was happening, he was on the floor with the bully on his back.

'Grab his head and rub his face in the dirt.'

Donald was struggling as hard as he could, but beginning to wail, as the other lad had hold of his ears. Our friends, taking advantage of the nearby park exit, had disappeared. I couldn't leave my brother, but I couldn't help him in a fist fight. Most of the people were out of sight, making their way to the exits nearer the town. I ran towards an American, still lying on the grass with a woman. He was about fifty yards away, but he was our only chance.

'Please help me. Them two big lads, up there near the gate, they're going to break my brother's arms because we won't give them our Railway Book. They're rubbing his face in the dirt.'

'Gee, kid, I'm always fighting somebody else's war. I won't be a minute, honey.'

He stood up and raced towards the bullies. By the time I reached them, he already had grabbed the two bullies by the scruff of the neck, pulling them effortlessly off Donald's back. Donald's shirt was torn and his face full of blood. The American looked at me. 'Hey, kid, which is your way home?'

Breathlessly, I pointed through the gates.

'Right, you two, on your way.'

He released the neck holds, and at the same time, with a firm push, sent the bullies in the opposite direction.

'Scram, fast!'

Donald looked a mess as he slowly got to his feet.

'How do you feel, kid? You look as if you've been in one of those trenches.'

My brother was crying.

'Listen, kids, get yourselves through those gates and home.'

'Would you like some gum, chum?' I asked.

He stared at me for a moment. I thought I'd said something wrong.

Suddenly, he laughed very loudly.

‘Gee, kid, that was just wonderful’. He put his hand in his pocket, and as well as the chewing gum collected earlier, we went home with a shilling each in our pockets.

During the next couple of days, I came to a brave decision. Having remembered saying to the American ‘Our Railway Book’, I decided to share it with my brother. Any trains he spotted could be underlined in red ink and mine in black. I reminded him constantly that red was like the blood on his face, so that when he underlined a train number he would remember that bully.

My brother was pleased just to share the book, and from that moment my Railway Book became ‘Our Railway Book’.

# Swings and a Roundabout

'The summers were long and sunny in those days…' Many of my childhood memories with my grandmother and grandfather really are of long, sunny days. This day was no exception, though it was an exceptional day.

We, that is several boys, at least one touching double figures, had nothing planned, but having nothing planned didn't mean having nothing to do. Days like this would often be spent in the park on the swings and roundabout.

It started in the normal way. We met on the field opposite our field, then, strolling and loitering, made our way into the park. Between us, we mustered three bottles of water; this was a precious commodity, as otherwise it would be almost two grasslands distance to the nearest free water pedestal. On reaching the swings and roundabout, several contests would immediately be suggested, challenges made and accepted.

One challenge I was never able to contest was the number of times the swing could be sent over the top bar. Despite innumerable attempts, I never got close to even "once over". But jumping off the swing and flying through the air was great fun. Just for that one exciting moment I couldn't breathe and my heart stopped. It was a wonderful and daring challenge. On landing, as if all in one motion, you bent double, tucked your chin tightly into your chest, and rolled forward on your shoulder in a curled-up ball. The real experts completed their go standing firmly on their two feet at the finish. It was exciting, especially when the contest became serious and you were straining for greater distance.

The roundabout was equally competitive, the main skills being either to jump on or jump off as it was whizzing round. When the roundabout had to be stopped, the normal procedure was to hold on to the side bar, using your feet as a brake;

sometimes you would be nearly horizontal, digging in your heels to slow down and stop the roundabout.

I was in that position when my grip on the side-rail failed, and, being already stretched out, I fell to the ground. Because of the continual "heeling" process the ground had been worn away, and my body landed in this inward-sloping gap. I was suddenly underneath the spinning roundabout, at the same time, being dragged round and further in. By the time it was stopped, I was stuck fast.

'Alan, are you all right?' said a voice.

I couldn't answer; I didn't know what had happened.

'Alan, can you speak?'

'I can't move,' I managed to reply.

A hand touched my body.

'Does anything hurt?' said a man's voice.

'No, but I'm stuck. Please don't move the roundabout.'

'Don't worry, lad. We'll get you out,' the voice said.

Despite their efforts, I still remained stuck.

'Listen, lad, somebody's gone for the fire brigade. We'll keep trying until they turn up.'

'I'll tell you something, lad, you're very brave…They won't be long now…You'll soon be free…They'll soon find out where you're stuck'…The encouragement was continuous, but it seemed ages until the firemen arrived. 'Right, lad, what's your name?'

'Alan.'

'Right, Alan, we'll soon have you free. We're going to loosen and clear away the ground all around you. This will give you more freedom. Let us know when you can move. We won't hurt you, and that's a promise. Is that clear, Alan?' said the fireman's friendly voice.

I suddenly felt better.

But after a few minutes careful picking, loosening and clearing, I was still stuck. It turned out that my clothes had become entangled with some of the bolted metal struts. The fireman couldn't manipulate me free, and had to cut my clothes free of the struts.

Quite a crowd had gathered to watch the firemen at work, and my dishevelled appearance from underneath that roundabout was greeted by loud cheers.

‘Well, lad, how do you feel?’ said this burly fireman. ‘I’m just going to check you for broken bones.’

‘I don’t feel so good.’ I looked at my ripped and filthy clothes. ‘I’ll never go on another roundabout.’

‘There you are, Alan,’ said another fireman. ‘Where do you live?’

He gave me a pear drop. I told him where I lived.

‘Right, lad, you’re OK,’ said the burly fireman. ‘Eee, you look as if you’ve just come out of the coal pit.’

‘Listen, Alan,’ said the second fireman, ‘let me see you walk slowly to our fire engine.’ This I did.

‘And how would you like to have a ride home?’

I nearly swallowed the pear drop. ‘Oh, yes, please.’

So the burly fireman lifted me into the front of the cab, and drove me home in style. When we arrived at Grandma’s house he lifted me down. It’s amazing how soon crowds gather. Before my feet had touched the ground, all the neighbours were staring and questioning the firemen. Grandma must have established that I wasn’t damaged, because she seemed pleased to be taking an important role in the proceedings. ‘This big fire engine brought him home and…’ would be familiar in future conversations. It was a tale to tell Grandad when he came home from his work. Grandma finally finished talking about the fire engine, and then Grandad had his say –

‘Eee, thar a rum lad.’

# Conkering

During those happy days being brought up by my grandma and grandad, I was involved in numerous scrapes. Our activities were sometimes foolish, often dangerous, though mishaps were not always my fault. During what should have been a pleasant pastime, I usually ended up suffering in one way or other. Take, for instance, the day my friend and I went conkering.

Peter was my age, but taller and stockier than I was. He was probably my best friend; whenever we fell out it seemed to upset me, whereas falling out with my other friends didn't.

'Have you got the nails?' he asked.

'Yes. Have you got the screws?'

'I've got seven.'

'I've got four nails, but they're long ones. Come on, let's get going.'

The direct route to the conker trees was along the side of the railway track. Being reasonably intelligent, we thought to kill two birds with one stone, so we put our nails and screws on the railway line to collect on the way back from conkering. By then, a train would have run over them, which would have resulted in the nails looking like knives and the screws looking like saw blades. These were always useful when it came to bartering for chewing gum or marbles.

Having placed the nails we established their position.

'It's near that big tree,' said Peter.

'There's too many trees; we'll forget which one.'

'I suppose you're right. Hey, why don't we pile up some stones on the path?'

'That's great. We'll not miss them.'

So we piled a large heap of stones in the middle of the path and continued to our main objective.

When we reached the conker trees it was obvious that someone had been there before us.

'Oh, look, Peter, at all the broken branches. I'll bet they've taken all the conkers.'

'I can't see any,' he said.

'Look at all the lumps of wood on the ground. They must have got loads of conkers,' I moaned. 'If only we'd come last week when I wanted to.'

'Let's throw some wood into the tree. We might hit some.'

We threw stones and lumps of wood into the dense and swaying mass of leaves in the hopeful off-chance of hitting a branch full of conkers. These futile attempts dampened our spirits. Then I had a bright idea. Being by far the lightest, if I stood on my friend's shoulders I could edge up the trunk and onto the lower branches, and then be able to loosen the conkers. It turned out to be easier than it looked.

I was already partly hidden from the watching Peter.

'Are you all right, Alan?'

'Yes, it was easy. But I can't see any conkers. I'll have to climb a bit further up.'

'Be careful. Can you not just shake the branch?' came Peter's distant voice.

'It's OK, it's not dangerous.'

After moving position in the dense foliage several times, I saw a great cluster of conkers dangling invitingly about three-quarters of the length of its branch from the trunk.

'Peter, There's some here. There's loads. I'll move along the branch and try to shake them loose.'

'Mind it doesn't break!'

'It won't break. Don't moider me, let me concentrate.'

I inched my way along the branch. Then…

'Peter, can you hear me?'

'Yes! What's wrong?'

'I'm stuck!'

'I'll try to climb up to help you.'

Time passed.

'Alan, it's no good. What are we going to do?'

'Listen, Peter. Go and get my grandad. Tell him I'm stuck high up in a conker tree. He'll know what to do. But listen, go round the back of our house. He'll be in the greenhouse.'

‘Right, I’m going now. Just stay there, don’t move.’

Stuck in that conker tree, I realised that whenever I was in trouble, I always turned to my grandma and grandad for help. Not far behind this thought was the feeling of increased peril. So much so that when my grandad arrived, it seemed that any movement, even breathing, might cause the branch to sway and me to fall. ‘Whereabouts are you, Alan?’ shouted Grandad.

Now frightened, I forced myself to answer him. Suddenly, the top of a ladder appeared. It rested firmly on the branch, between me and the tree trunk.

‘I can’t move, Grandad.’

‘Hang on, I’m climbing up.’

‘Don’t shake the branch, Grandad, or I’ll fall off.’

His strong arms lifted me off the branch and held me safe as he climbed back down. When he placed me on the ground, I couldn’t stand up, and my fingers wouldn’t move from the half-closed position. Grandad was extremely agitated and was struggling to breathe. Together we must have looked a sorry sight.

He was the first to come to, and then disappeared up the ladder again. The branches started to shake, and suddenly it was raining conkers. This speeded up my recovery.

On the way home, Grandad held the front of the ladder while Peter and I held the rear end, with our pockets stuffed with conkers. The pile of stones in the middle of the path reminded my grandad he had a complaint.

‘What silly fool piled up them stones? I nearly broke my neck coming up here. It’s a good job I didn’t, Alan, or else you’d still be up that tree.’

Peter and I said nothing, and neither did we look for or even mention those nails and screws.

# Alan McCracken
## The Threpny Bit Murderer

One of those twelve-sided three penny pieces, or "threpny bits" as people used to call them, once gave me a lot of scary trouble.

That day I set off for school with a spring in each step, carrying my satchel, gas mask and a threepenny bit.

It was easy to roll a penny; I could roll a penny further than the length of the longest cricket pitch. A threepenny bit was a different test – much more difficult. I struggled, without much success, trying different techniques, from standing to kneeling, at varying speeds. After one such futile attempt to roll this threepenny bit, I managed to lose it, and spent so long looking for it that I lost track of time. After trying my usually reliable techniques of judging estimated speed and distance, angle of trajectory and arc of throwing stance, eventually I gave up my threepenny bit as lost.

The spring in my step had also gone, as I trudged miserably to school, having just lost at least two Horlicks tablets and a penny drink. I had gone about three quarters of the way to school when I sensed something was different. The streets, normally filled at this time with children, were silent. I was late. I had never been late for school before. And how late? At least thirty minutes, it seemed. Not going to school at all would be better than facing the headmaster.

So I decided to stay out of sight of people and streets. We were lucky, living within about half an hour of the countryside, with lots of woodland, rhododendron shrubbery, pathways, streams and small glades leading to open fields.

I made my way out of the familiar streets where I may have been recognised. Though with no plan and no food, I walked along whistling, happy in the strange experience of actually playing truant. The prospect of a lovely day looking for birds' nests and exploring lay in front of me.

My whistling stopped, and so did my jaunty step, at a field. There in front of me was a bull. It looked fierce, with wide, staring eyes. Nothing would make me enter that field. I skirted cautiously round the hedge, the bull on the other side of the ditch, staring menacingly at me through the gaps.

Safely further on, I scrambled to the top of a wooded rise. It looked down to a stream, which had boulders and large stones that you could jump across. This is where I saw him.

"Wanted for murder".

I had seen that face, that bald-headed, drooping face in the local police station window. This face was jumping across the boulders. He saw me, staring at him. He shouted something that sounded like, 'Come here, you.' That woke me up. Stumbling back down the incline, frightened and leaden-footed, I heard him shout again, but only the sound; the words were indistinct. I jumped over the stile and made for a gap in the hedge – straight into the bull's field. The bull, though, was no longer the danger. So, across the field, then a frantic scramble into and out of the ditch, through another gap in the hedge, to safety, from the bull at least.

The murderer was standing at the stile, looking across the field at me. Glad now of the bull in the field, I disappeared into the shrubbery, deeper and deeper into the densest and safest place, and sat still and breathless, surrounded by unfamiliar bird cries and quiet rustling. I listened intently for the sound of crunching feet. Thankfully, nothing happened. I kept very still, hardly daring to breathe, knowing that at some point I would have to leave my hideaway, and wishing I had never tried to roll that threepenny bit.

It seems strange to me now, but at this point I opened my school satchel and started to read my library book. It was called "The Speckled Egg", and there was some similarity in the story to my own plight. The hen was trying her best to hatch little chicks, but every time she laid an egg it was a speckled one. Speckled eggs just happened to be the farmer's favourite, so the egg disappeared, and the hen had to start all over again. She had to find a place where the speckled eggs would be safe. I was like that speckled egg; I needed to be safe. In the story, the hen finally found an ingenious hiding place, and eventually strutted through the farmyard proudly showing off her little chicks. This book helped me through my ordeal.

The point eventually arrived when I felt able to move, flitting from cover to cover, and running as fast as I could over the open ground until houses and people came into view.

When the streets became more familiar, I slowed down, hardly able to breathe. By the time I approached our field, I had just about recovered, but felt like crying. It had been a horrible experience. Every time I hear those words, 'Come here, you,' I think of the murderer.

I was only half an hour later home than normal. This was not quite long enough for my grandma to become worried, and it was a wonderful feeling to hear her voicing, her disapproval over my lateness. All my chores, plus extra, were done voluntarily, with great gusto that evening.

I have rolled pennies since then, but have never again played truant.

# Walking Day

Those happy years staying with my grandma and grandad meant going to a church school, where there were regular Sunday walking days. The walkers had to be organised and arranged, and if the walk took half an hour, we seemed to be standing and waiting to be "placed" for twice that long. The more important the walk, the longer the placing took. The May festival and the Whit Sunday walks were the big turnouts.

On one of these days, we took the opportunity to prove our skill with a new invention – the pea gun. It wasn't actually new, in that we had been using them for a while, but "open war" in front of adults and leering children on the Walking Day streets had never been done before.

The gun, with a movable wooden square block tied up in a strategic position by elastic bands, could flick a dried pea a reasonable distance with a fairly good chance of it going in the direction the barrel was pointing. The main skill would not be firing the gun, but loading it whilst walking down the open street.

'The pea gun's no good. Everybody will see us loading it.'

'What else can we use?'

'We'll just have to walk and pull faces at them.'

Nobody seemed to have a suggestion. Occasionally, I was the one to come forward with a bright idea, and the use of the pea gun on the Walking Day was just one of these. It was obvious that some distraction was required so the public gaze would be diverted away from us. The way forward would be to position ourselves as close to the brass band as possible. Unless, of course, I could get out of the walk completely.

'Right, Alan, it's a special day today, one of them big walks, so I want you looking extra clean and smart in your best suit.'

'Oh, grandma, some of my friends are just watching. They said they're too old to –'

‘Who said that? I’ll speak to their mothers about this.’

‘I can’t remember, it was ages ago. They said nobody looks at the walkers anyway, they just watch the band, even when they’re not playing.’

I wished I hadn’t complained, as grandma was becoming impatient.

‘Listen, Alan, it’s a big Walking Day, and I want to see you in the procession, so go and get ready.’

So, with grandma firmly and finally establishing her position and my role in the day’s proceedings, it would be important that I stationed myself as close as possible to the band. This would provide maximum opportunity for the loading of the pea gun. If it came down to “every man for himself”, then to sneak into that prime position would be my target. Luckily, several of us were placed perfectly.

The walk started, and immediately I began to select my targets. Any watching boy or girl who laughed or pulled faces at me would get a shot from the pea gun. I managed to fire a number of telling shots. Although they didn’t know what had hit them, their laughing faces suddenly changed, looking painfully vexed and bewildered, instant proof of a direct hit, and a further notch on my gun.

I discovered later that none of the other boys had found enough courage or skill to reload their pea guns. All my planning and practising had paid off, and the walk had been fun after all.

This walk was important enough to conclude with an organised field day. This was mainly a “get together”, where grown-ups would meet other grown-ups they hadn’t seen since the same walk the previous year. At least the church community kept in touch. People would stand or sit on the grass, laughing and talking, telling tales that could easily have happened nearly one year ago. We, the young ones, were allowed to run wild.

The one organised event which gave everybody a chance to circulate, be involved, and perhaps meet other members of the church community was the one which I decided to try. The instructions were simple enough: ‘Hidden somewhere are three blocks of wood, each block being two inches wide and twelve inches in length; they are painted green and numbered one, two or three in yellow. If you find one of these blocks of wood, then come to this tent, and inside the tent, you can exchange the block for a mystery prize.'

Having listened carefully to these instructions, I ran excitedly over to my grandma and grandad, who were sitting happily on the grass with some people I had never seen before.

'Grandma, can I go and look for a green-painted block of wood? If I find it, I'll win a prize!'

'What's the prize?' asked Grandad.

'I don't know, it's a mystery.'

'All right, but don't get up to any mischief, and remember where you are and where we are,' said Grandma.

'All right, Grandma.'

'Listen, Alan, if you find a green-painted block of wood, bring it over here and let me have a look at it.' Grandad was chuckling to himself.

So off I went. And "off I went" is definitely what I did, becoming completely engrossed in the excitement. As I drifted in my quest for treasure, and paying little attention to where I was going, the Walking Day field vanished, and my enthusiasm for the search also began to fade. It was the unusual silence that finally stopped my wandering tracks. Filled with alarm, I forgot the wooden treasure, and my attention began to focus on finding out where I was. I scrambled to the summit of the nearest big hill; the view from the top showed clearly that four fields separated me from my distant grandparents.

Breathless from the uphill exertion, but less panicky, I set off at my fastest pace, weaving my way through hedges and ditches. The faint cries of children playing grew louder with every field crossed. When I reached the Walking Day field, nothing had changed; it seemed just as full as before I left. My grandma and grandad were still sitting on the grass, talking quietly with several other people.

'Why, it's Alan. Where have you been, lad? It's over an hour since the last green piece of wood was found. I said to your grandma: it's a mystery what that lad gets up to.'

I just mumbled something about playing and running about.

'You won't want your tea, now you've had something to eat,' said Grandma. 'It's been a lovely quiet day, and they did well, giving us all some cake and biscuits. I think they should have more field day get-togethers. We can all sit down and talk, and Alan can run about and play, and there's no danger of him getting lost.'

'Yes, Polly, these field days are good,' said Grandad. 'Especially,' he continued, looking at me with a knowing smile, 'when you get free cakes and biscuits.'

# Fishing

In Grandma's words: 'That was completely and utterly thoughtless stupidity.'

This day was invitingly sunny. It was Sunday, which meant dressing up in my best suit, shirt, tie and polished shoes before trekking off to Sunday School at eleven o'clock. It lasted for 45 minutes, so by half-past one, I had been to Sunday School, walked home, had dinner and was ready to play.

'Can I go out to play, Grandma?'

'No, you're not playing out today; your auntie's coming this afternoon, and I want her to see you in your best suit.'

'Can I not go fishing? I'll just be sat there. I won't be playing with anybody.'

'Who are you going fishing with?'

'Nobody, Grandma. I'll just sit down by myself and try and catch a fish. Please.'

'It's a nice day, and nothing can happen, can it?'

She finally relented, on the basis that my fishing consisted in standing or sitting, and remained completely free of any boisterous activity.

The pond was next to our field, on the other side of the railway line. It was simple – under the railway bridge, walk about thirty paces, then squirm either on my back or stomach, through the gap under the railings which guarded the pond. The dryness of the day meant that I could easily dust down my clothes.

I was ready for fishing, with one of my grandad's longest garden canes partly prepared for use, with black cotton and a bent pin attached. I had some worms, lead weights and matchsticks in tins. Ready for my catch was a jam jar held with string.

Finding a good place to sit and fish was easy, and with the float and worm quickly attached, I was soon casting out a good distance, thanks to Grandad's extra-long cane. It was a lovely day. Nothing seemed to be moving except dragonflies and insects. The pond faded into a coloured haze under the dreamy sun; only the occasional tremor of the rod brought me to my senses with the rising elation that a fish was biting, before I sank back into drowsiness.

Then the unbelievable happened; my matchstick quill started to quiver, then went under, gone in a flash. My instant delight was short-lived, as almost immediately, a sudden jerk on the cane pulled me off my feet and into the water, head first. It was only then that I lost control of the cane completely; it slid from my grasp and travelled at some speed towards the middle of the pond, leaving me scrambling out of the now murky water.

For some time afterwards, I lay in the sunshine in the forlorn hope that my best suit would dry out, wondering why the cotton line hadn't broken. This, though, was only a delaying tactic, for the awful journey home had to be made. It was impossible to cover up this disaster; Grandma would eventually see the mess, made even worse with clinging wet dust as I went back under the railings. If I sneaked up the stairs and changed, she would immediately want to know what was going on.

Anyway, probably because she had one ear at the door with relatives expected, my grandma heard me enter the house. I can see her grim face now, as she strides towards me, stripping and smacking, smacking and stripping, repeating and repeating, 'That was completely and utterly thoughtless stupidity.' Finally, completely naked, I was banished to the bedroom. It seems funny how certain things stick in your mind; during the stripping and smacking, it struck me vividly that I was glad my relatives had not yet arrived to see my grandma at work.

By teatime, she had relented, and I was shouted down to meet the relatives, wearing my clean Monday school clothes. During tea, which was always "something special" when we had relatives, Grandad was his normal self; he never seemed to let things fade.

'Alan, after tea, will you bring out my long canes from the back of the shed? There should be exactly thirty.'

'And don't have a mark on those clothes, or else you're in for it,' warned Grandma.

'Right, Grandma.'

During my tea, I struggled with the problem of thirty, but had no solution.

After tea, Grandad came outside and sat on his wicker chair watching me count. Worriedly, I pretended to look for the thirtieth cane.

He lit his pipe and puffed contentedly.

'I suppose twenty-nine will do,' he said.

I sank back in relief.

Ruffling my hair, he looked at me with a smile.

'Eee, thar a rum lad.'

# Bonfire Night

The first bonfire I remember was in our field. We had been collecting wood every weekend for ages. To start with, people turned us away – 'Come back when it's nearer the time' – but over the impatient weeks, the stack grew and grew.

Some of the bonfire collectors were busy every night, but in the winter time, except on special occasions, I was not allowed to play out in the dark. Collecting bonfire wood was not deemed by my grandma to be a special occasion, so my contribution was limited to the weekend. In the daylight hours, we picked our spot, usually at the corner of our field, taking turns to sit with a "penny for the guy". Any money collected was stored in a biscuit tin for a share-out on bonfire day.

As the time came closer, I grew more and more excited. At some point very soon, Grandma would have to be approached. I had two hurdles to cross before the bonfire was to be lit by a responsible adult at 6:30.

'Eee, Grandma, it's been hard collecting wood for our bonfire.'

'Where have you got all that wood from? We could have done with some of that.'

Grandma wasn't showing any indications of sympathy. I would have to face the first hurdle head on.

'Err, Grandma, can I watch the bonfire being lit? It's only on our field, and I'll know everybody.'

Almost over the first hurdle.

'All right, Alan. Keep with the grown-ups.'

'Thanks, Grandma. Can I set off my fireworks as well? There'll only be a few jumping jacks, some Catherine wheels and some sparklers.'

'You're not setting fireworks off. They're too dangerous.'

‘Mr Whitaker said he’d set them off for me, if you didn’t mind.’

I definitely hadn’t to be cheeky, whatever my grandma said.

‘Where have you got money to buy daft fireworks?’

‘It’s the penny for the guy money, Grandma. We’re sharing it out on bonfire day.’

‘Are you sure Mr Whitaker said he would set them off?’

‘Yes, Grandma.’ I felt hopeful. ‘He said if you let him, he’ll set them off for me.’

‘Go on, then, but stand well away from him when he lights them.’

‘Oh, thanks, Grandma. I can’t wait for bonfire night.’

‘But one hour is enough for you around that bonfire, so be back in here for half past seven. A good wash and straight off to bed. Do you understand, Alan?’

Normally our home time when playing out in the light evenings was seven o’clock, so my grandma was being very good to allow me to stay out half an hour later, and in the dark.

‘Oh, yes, I promise I won’t be late.’

The second hurdle wasn’t quite cleared, but I forced myself to wait until the last moment, when the share-out took place. Thanks to Guy Fawkes and Holmes’ corner shop, my money became six jumping jacks, six Catherine wheels and twenty sparklers.

I didn’t have the nerve to ask my grandma if I could set off the sparklers, just in case she changed her mind about letting me go to the bonfire. It was time for a bit of ingenuity.

‘Grandma, will you show me how they sparkle?’ I had never seen one lit before.

‘All right, Alan, just come into the backyard and I’ll set one going.’

She looked pleased. When it started to sparkle, I hopefully held out my hand. It worked. She gave me the sparkler and watched me happily spray sparkles in all directions. Grandma smiled.

‘Right, Grandma, it’s nearly half past six. I’ll be back for half past seven. Oh, when Mr Whitaker lights the sparklers, can I hold them?’

Moments later, a happy seven year old was running down the garden path having successfully cleared his second hurdle.

The time finally arrived. The field looked crowded, but for some reason, everyone was on one side of our massive bonfire. One of our neighbours, looking important, set the bonfire alight. As if by magic the fire took hold, and within seconds, the flames were spitting and cracking, and hissing and shooting sparks, covering a great area, all on the opposite side from the gaping crowd. That would not have been a good place to be standing.

Guy Fawkes, standing clearly and defiantly, remained visible only for a short time before, accompanied by a great cheer from the crowd, he disappeared, sadly for me, into the crackling flames and smoke.

It was like a big party. People who had never been known to smile now looked happy.

Mr Whitaker lit my first sparkler and placed it in my eager hands; the starry patterns fascinated me, even when the last fluttering spark petered out.

The Catherine wheels, nailed onto some nearby trees, had the same kind of fascination. The jumping jacks were just fun. The women, and there seemed to be a great number, screamed and jumped if a firework moved sharply in their direction, not like the men, who tried to kick it towards them. The unpredictability of the jumping jacks meant that often they leapt back with a bang towards the men, giving the ladies a chance to laugh. The time passed like the flash of one of the many rockets zooming from milk bottles into the dark sky, to burst in a cascade of colour. I thought they would fall like bombs and land on our heads.

So my extra half-hour passed; time to go home. As I trudged away, I heard the talk of black peas and hotpot. I had already spent time at the bonfire eating lots of treacle toffee, given out by a friendly old lady, knitting behind a table. But black peas and hotpot sounded good.

'Well, Alan, have you had a good time?' asked Grandma.

'It's been the most exciting thing I've ever seen, Grandma. The jumping jacks were really funny. It looked as if the flames and sparks would touch the sky. Thank you for letting me hold the sparklers and for letting me stay out late.'

'Right, hurry up, it's time for a really good wash and off to bed,' Grandad chipped in impatiently.

This was strange coming from Grandad. It was usually Grandma who ushered me off to bed.

On the short walk back home from the bonfire, with black peas and hotpot ringing in my ears, I had come to a decision. With the living room door closed, and it would be, to stop the draught, Grandma and Grandad wouldn't hear me creep back out of the house. I would get the black peas and the hotpot, and take them back to my bedroom.

Sneaking out was a slow process. Not a sound. If caught, my excuse would be that the treacle toffee had made me thirsty, and I was coming down for a drink of water.

'But lad, why are you in your clothes? Why are you not in your pyjamas?'

'The flames and sparks from the bonfire might set fire to our house. If they do, I can run out quicker because I'm already dressed.'

These reasons sounded very convincing to me. But they weren't needed. Out of the house I crept, down the garden path, through the open gate and out onto the field. Just a small distance to my left was the bonfire, now more peaceful. The crowd had settled into small, quieter groups around the glowing fire, their shadowy faces hard to see clearly in the glare.

Being on familiar territory, I was able to manoeuvre easily, stopping occasionally to watch a banger or a rocket being set off. Despite these distractions, my only objective was those black peas and hotpot.

Suddenly, something grabbed me around the waist, at the same time lifting me off the ground. A fierce pain at the back of my neck increased as I was dragged away from the bonfire.

Through the gate, up the stairs, and finally flung onto the bed. No words had been spoken. It all happened so fast; it was only as I was being yanked up the garden path that I realised that my grandad was the cause of all this pain.

I wasn't to know that my grandma and grandad had joined in the later celebrations, those in the form of black peas and hotpot. I had been spotted and dealt with accordingly.

This obviously didn't spoil their night. When Grandad came home from work the following day, all he said was, 'Eee, them black peas and hotpot were good.'

# Blackpool

'Hello, Alan! Come and sit down and listen.'

These words filled me with alarm. Grandma's request to "come and sit down and listen" always preceded words of a very serious and important nature.

'OK, Grandma.'

'Don't say OK like them Americans; that's slang. You must learn to talk properly. Now, how would you like to go on a holiday to Blackpool?'

In answering this question, I didn't say OK; in fact, momentarily unable to speak, all I managed was a startled yes.

'You've been a very good boy, and the war is nearly over, so your grandad is being given a week's holiday. He said why don't we all go to Blackpool? That'll be nice, won't it? I think we could have a spoonful of malt now.'

I ate the malt in silence, savouring the moment and thinking about this surprise, before peppering Grandma with lots of questions, most of which were answered by 'Ask your grandad'.

That evening, I couldn't contain my excitement; instead of waiting on the bottom stair, I met my grandad at the point where he entered our field.

'Grandad, Grandma says we're going to Blackpool!'

'When?'

Grandad always seemed to be able to stop me in my tracks. In this instant, just the word 'When?' was enough to sow a seed of doubt in my mind.

'She told me today when I got home from school. She said that you said, "Why don't we all go to Blackpool?"'

'But what about my tomatoes?'

'Mr Whitaker could water them.'

‘Eee, Alan, thar a rum lad. Well, come on then, let’s have our tea and talk about it. Let’s see what Grandma’s been telling everybody.’

The first day of our holiday finally came. Grandad carried our large suitcase on his shoulder, down the garden path and across our field to the bus stop, talking with great enthusiasm.

‘Eee, this brings back some memories! It feels as if I’m carrying my kitbag, except this case isn’t as heavy.’

When we reached the bus stop, I tried to lift the suitcase, but couldn’t even budge it. Donald and I each had a very small brown suitcase for our swimming trunks and towels. Tied to my suitcase was a bucket and spade. The bus to Wigan arrived and my excitement grew. I was soon to experience one of the thrills of my lifetime.

By the time we arrived at the railway station, I was struggling to breathe. This wasn’t an asthma attack; it was just an attack of fever-pitch excitement. Grandad bought two and two halves to Blackpool return. The ticket collector clipped the tickets and directed us to the right platform, which was crowded with holidaymakers. Grandad seemed to know everybody. Suddenly, there came a piercing whistle, followed by a deafening noise and a blast of wind and smoke. “Th’express!” Momentarily, my excitement was replaced by fright, which found me holding on tightly to Grandma for safety. Then came another sound, this time human-like, resonating from the public address system, a sound which seemed impossible to understand. I was filled with admiration for Grandad when he immediately clarified the mumblings as being ‘The next train is for Blackpool’.

I looked down the line, feet firmly planted, one yard from the edge of the platform, obediently heeding Grandma’s warning. The train appeared in the distant haze, slowly moving closer until it finally came, hissing and gasping, to a creaking, complaining halt. By this time, I was positioned at my grandma’s “request”, six feet from the platform edge. I was goggle-eyed. It was massive, too big to take in. The experience was so overwhelming, both going and coming back, that I completely forgot to write down the name and number of any trains.

We entered our compartment, self-contained third class, with no corridor. The only opening window was in the door, and slid up and down, retained in position by a three-inch wide leather strap. Donald and I were the only children in the compartment; I sat on Grandad's knee or stood near the closed window. Before the train moved off, and at each station, I was allowed to open the window using the leather strap. I found out very quickly that the weight of the window had to be held or it would crash down, out of control. When this happened to me in Wigan station, I was faced with a compartment full of fixed disapproval. Grandad came to the rescue by showing me the correct way to open the window, so that when we finally approached our destination, I felt competent and confident in my ability. This was acknowledged within the compartment, now full of nodding approval.

The train pulled slowly into the safety of Blackpool Central. Throwing caution to the wind and, in daredevil fashion, just like the Americans when the troop trains passed our field, I leaned my head out of the open window, trying to catch the eyes of the waiting people. The platform was crowded.

The very moment that our feet touched the ground, a smart-looking porter approached.

'Carry your bags, sir? It's a long walk to the exit and your bags look heavy.'

He was very polite and courteous.

'That's all right, lad. It's only a light weight; it's not like my kitbag.'

Grandad's answer had been very pleasant and good-humoured, but the displeased porter turned away abruptly to look for a more willing customer.

'You can carry my suitcase,' I said, feeling slightly sorry for him. He looked towards Grandad, who was now absorbed in hoisting the suitcase onto his shoulder.

The porter took this opportunity to direct his annoyance towards me.

'Get lost, kid. I hope it rains all week.' He then disappeared into the milling crowd.

I picked up my suitcase quickly and followed Grandad. We passed the steaming engine, massive and magnificent. I felt that I could look at it for ever. The complaining and gasping had ceased. Its job, to haul hundreds of holidaymakers to the other side of the world, had been successfully completed, and it was now resting majestically; except for an occasional short sigh, it remained completely still and silent.

'Come on, Alan,' said Grandma. 'Keep up with your grandad. We can't stand staring at trains all week.'

'It's so big and strong and powerful, Grandma. I've never been this close to a train before. I wish I could climb up there,' pointing excitedly at the engine compartment.

'Right, Alan, come on or you'll get lost.' Grandma had had enough.

We joined the queue and moved towards the ticket collector. Then, over the indecipherable loudspeakers, I heard, for the first time since our arrival, other trains making the now familiar hissing, gasping and complaining sounds. I suddenly felt scared to find myself in the middle of such bustling activity, and stood close to Grandma, holding her hand tightly until we passed the ticket collector and moved out of the station.

Our guest house was only a five minute walk from the station. Grandad, suitcase on his shoulder, led the way, followed by Grandma, carrying her handbag and a shopping basket; followed by me, carrying my small suitcase and bucket and spade, with strict instructions from my grandma not to lag behind; at the rear, also carrying his suitcase, was Donald, with his own orders: not to let me dawdle. This allowed Donald to regularly clip my heels on the pretence that I was too slow, and that I must heed Grandma's warning and keep up. It didn't matter, because nothing could spoil my brimming excitement on this wonderful day.

We arrived at the guest house, freshly painted in pale yellow. There were two or three signs in the window, one of which read *No Vacancies*.

'What does "No Vacancies" mean, Grandad?'

'Full up,' said Grandad, panting from his efforts.

This answer left me thinking he wasn't very hungry. Yet almost immediately after our arrival, we found ourselves sitting around a large table with other new guests, having what Grandad, who I thought was full up, called "a slap-up meal". Later, my grandma explained the meaning of "no vacancies".

'Eee, this is the life,' Grandad exclaimed, sinking heavily into a comfortable-looking armchair in our rooms. 'Nothing to do, and all day to do it in. When I've got my breath back and smoked a pipe, we'll go on to the Golden Mile.'

I thought he must have got his breath back in order to eat that slap-up meal.

'What's the Golden Mile, Grandad?'

'You'll see in a minute, lad.'

'Is it where the rainbow ends? Have we arrived at the end of the rainbow?' I was unable to contain my impatience.

'It feels like it. It's going to be a wonderful holiday,' said Grandma, sighing with pleasure.

I had never seen her looking so relaxed and happy.

'While Grandad's having a pipe, I'll empty the suitcase into the drawers and wardrobe. Donald, you and Alan please take your clothes into your bedroom and put them all away neatly.' This was one facet of my grandma that was instantly recognisable.

It took about an hour for Grandad to recover. Most of this time he spent in the armchair, smoking his pipe. I managed to remain patient, despite my heart beating "twenty to the dozen", as my grandma would say. At last, Grandad could breathe and we finally departed the guest house.

Within five minutes, we had reached the sea front. Grandma was eager.

'Come on, Grandad, let's see the sea, the tide's in.'

I was puzzled, being unable to grasp what "the tide's in" meant.

'Right, Polly, let's cross the road.'

It was the widest and busiest road I had ever seen, with a fast-moving stream of horses and carts, horses and carriages, motor cars, buses and trams. Having successfully crossed, we finally faced the sea. It was a lovely, calm and warm sunny afternoon, but the sea was battering the barrier which my grandad called the sea wall. We were on top of the sea wall looking down, my grandma holding me back with two hands. The sea seemed to me to be seething, frothing, angry and dangerous, and stretched further than I could see. It felt as if we were standing on the very edge of the world.

I managed to say, 'Grandma, where can I make sandcastles and sand pies?'

'Underneath all that water, there's some sand; you can play in that.'

Grandad had to raise his voice to be heard.

Grandma smiled at Grandad, then took my hand and led me to the relative safety and silence afforded us by one of the many shelters placed a short distance from the sea wall.

'When the tide's in all that sea water rushes in towards the sea wall and covers all the sand. But when the tide goes out, the sea moves away from the sea wall and then Grandad can sit on his deckchair and you can build sandcastles. Don't be frightened, Alan; when the sea is hitting the sea wall, it's deep and dangerous, but it only comes towards the sea wall slowly, so we're given enough warning.'

By this time, Grandad had come into the shelter, and he added his comforting words.

'You just build sandcastles and make sand pies, lad. I won't leave you stranded like Robinson Crusoe.'

I hadn't read Robinson Crusoe, but I knew he was marooned on a desert island, surrounded by water.

'When does the tide go out?' This question was directed at both grandparents.

'When you see the sand,' said Grandad, sounding very clever, 'what you do, lad, is look over the sea wall and you either see the sea or you see the sand.' Then, with a contented sigh, 'Well, who wants to see the Golden Mile?'

'Oh, yes, please, Grandad.'

'It's over there', he said, pointing across the busy road.

I had started this first day of our holiday in a trance; now I was puzzled.

Grandad did nothing to enlighten me, seeming so matter-of-fact.

'Let's cross the road and we'll go on the Golden Mile.'

'Grandma, will you please tell me where the rainbow is? I want to see the gold.'

'Alan, this is a test. What do you see over there? I'll help you to start – what do you see that's moving?'

'I see lots of people. There are soldiers, sailors, pilots.' I thought everybody in the RAF was a pilot. 'There are some Americans with girlfriends. And I can see people like us, Grandma.'

'Have they anything in common?' she asked.

'What do you mean, Grandma?' I said anxiously, feeling the golden prize slipping away.

'Well, Alan,' she said, very patiently, 'when you look at one person, then another, or even a whole group – what is one person doing that another person is doing, that you see all the group doing?' Grandma had nearly told me the answer.

'They're all smiling, Grandma! They are all people with happy faces!'

'Well, Alan, that's the Golden Mile. When you go on the Golden Mile everybody is smiling, everybody is happy. It's as if they've all had a huge spoonful of malt.'

'What happens when you reach the end of the Golden Mile? Is everybody sad?'

'No, lad,' said Grandad. 'When you reach the end of the Golden Mile, you reach the Pleasure Beach, and that's when the fun and games start.'

I crossed the road utterly perplexed.

We entered the Golden Mile, and spent the rest of that first afternoon drifting among fortune tellers, side shows and penny arcades, ignoring those people grandad called "spivs", who were, apparently, "still up to their tricks".

We were smiling, we were happy, we were part of the Golden Mile.

Filtering through the hubbub and the squealing of the spivs came the news – 'Tide's going out.' This seemed to raise everybody's spirits even higher. It also set me thinking: if, when the tide goes out, what if the sea doesn't disappear, and me and Donald could play on the beach and also paddle in the water? 'Grandma, does the sea disappear when the tide goes out?'

'It does at Southport,' said Grandad.

'No, Alan, it doesn't disappear. In fact, when we go on the beach tomorrow, you and Donald can make sandcastles and run and paddle in the sea. You'll have a lovely time.'

I thought about this, and then, as we were making our way back to the guest house for our tea, threw caution to the wind.

'Grandma, can me and Donald go for a swim after our tea?'

'Don't be silly, Alan. You know very well you can't swim,' she replied pleasantly.

‘It’s not tea, it’s dinner,’ interrupted Grandad, trying to look clever.

‘What do you mean, it’s dinner?’ I answered, feeling a little peeved at the interruption. ‘Dinner’s in the middle of the day. Grandma always says, “Come on, Alan, it’ll soon be dinner time, set the table.”’

‘Not when you’re in Blackpool. In Blackpool, dinner is lunch and tea is dinner.’

Grandad seemed to be showing off.

‘What do you mean, Grandad? If dinner is lunch and tea is dinner, what’s an evening meal?’

‘What do you mean, an evening meal?’ Grandad asked, somewhat irritated.

‘Well, on the guest house window, it says “Evening meals provided”.’

‘Come on, Polly, let’s get back to the digs for our tea – I’m starving.’

‘But, Grandad, I thought you said tea was dinner in Blackpool.’

Suddenly, there was a change from ambling to fast walking, and me running to keep up, listening to Grandma’s last words – ‘Don’t try to be clever with your grandad, especially when he’s starving.’

So, even though I was tempted to call dinner lunch and tea dinner, I wasn’t daring enough. I followed Grandma’s instructions, and throughout the entire holiday, I called them dinner and tea, like my grandad.

We reached the guest house in what was probably the entire holiday’s record time. Grandad’s attitude now changed. Evening meal, dinner, tea, it didn’t matter. It was another slap-up meal.

‘Where have they got all the food coupons from, Grandma? It’s twice as much as you give me.’

‘From the black market,’ said Grandad, once again sounding clever. Now, with a massive meal in front of him, his voice and entire manner glowed with contentment.

‘What’s – ’

I didn’t finish the sentence. Grandma’s face was like thunder. Whether it was caused by my reference to the limited quantity of food we received at home – due to war rationing – or being too clever with Grandad, her warning glare silenced me.

For the rest of the meal, I said nothing, and tried my hardest to be on my best behaviour.

Shortly afterwards, having settled in our rooms, everything was peaceful. Grandad was in the comfortable armchair, smoking his pipe and reading a newspaper, while Grandma rearranged the clothes into different drawers and wardrobes.

I took the chance to broach the subject again.

'Grandma, I didn't really mean a swim. I meant just to run along the beach and make sandcastles and paddle at the edge of the world.'

Grandma was silent.

At this point, Donald came to the rescue, as usual.

'Grandma, please let us. I'll look after Alan. It's only two streets to the Golden Mile road, and I know where to cross over to the beach safely,' he pleaded.

'I'll do everything Donald tells me, and we'll be back by half past eight.'

Grandma was wavering.

'While we're on the beach, you and Grandad can have a rest, and then get all poshed up and go downstairs for a quiet drink,' said Donald, now sounding less pleading, but more persuasive.

My grandad had already pointed out to us that going downstairs for a drink would necessitate their entering the room "all poshed up". Grandma would wear a floral-patterned pale cotton dress and plain, darker cardigan. Grandad would wear a charcoal-grey three-piece suit; his jacket remained forever unfastened, and his waistcoat, partly buttoned up, would allow him to display proudly his silver pocket watch and chain. Whenever I saw my grandad in his charcoal-grey three-piece suit, I always thought he looked "posh".

Donald's persuasive technique was good, but something else was needed.

'Grandma, we could take our suitcases with us so when we get changed, we can put our good new clothes into them and keep them clean and free from the sand. If the sand is wet, our clothes will stay dry.' I thought it best to cover everything in order to strengthen our case.

Although she didn't look completely certain, Grandma relented.

So that Saturday evening after our tea, the two of us set off, clasping each other's hands tightly and carrying our suitcases. As we entered the edge of the Golden Mile, we closed our eyes to the immediate magnetic attractions displayed all around us. I probably looked excited, but the necessity of holding Donald's hand even more tightly than usual revealed my true feelings, that is, frightened. Donald was looking equally excited, but he had volunteered responsibility for me, in what for both of us was a new and potentially dangerous situation.

'Listen, Alan, please do everything I say.' He sounded anxious.

'OK, Donald.' It was safe to say OK, being out of earshot of my grandma.

'Well, the main thing is to hold my hand while we're on the Golden Mile.'

'OK, Donald.'

We both gained comfort and confidence from holding hands. Donald led me safely across the wide, busy road and onto the beach. The beach, to my amazement, looked deserted. I let go of Donald's hand, and we both ran, skipped, jumped and raced in wild freedom, until eventually collapsing contentedly onto the soft sand.

'I'm going for a swim,' said Donald breathlessly.

'So am I.'

'You can't swim,' he taunted.

'I can swim in the sea, because the sea is full of salt and salt helps you to float.'

'It's not salt, it's brine.'

His knowledgeable answer seemed to please Donald up to a point, though at the back of his mind would have been his promise to look after me.

'Well, let's get changed and see what happens,' he said dubiously.

So we quickly took off our new clothes, putting them untidily into the suitcases. Now wearing just our swimming trunks, and with any fear of danger fading fast, we dashed towards the water's edge. Donald didn't stop. He ran gleefully into the water until he was swimming, leaving me cowering and shivering, ankle-deep in the water.

'Come on, Alan! It's wonderful!'

'I'm scared.'

'Come on! Just flap your arms and legs, and pretend to be swimming.'

I moved hesitantly forward. Slowly, the water grew deeper and my body became less. When I reached Donald, the water was above my swimming trunks and I was beginning to lose control of my feet, which seemed to want to move upwards.

'Donald, please help me to swim.'

'Listen, you need to put your head under the water to get used to it.'

'I can't.'

'Well, I'll help you.' Donald's enthusiasm had overcome any fear; he helped me by scooping sea water up and over my face, then swimming quickly away, shrieking with laughter.

But, slipping and floundering, I lost my balance and sank, my head disappearing under the water. I was a delicate little boy, and, managing only feeble resistance, was quickly swallowing sea water. Struggling unsuccessfully to recover my balance, now feeling suddenly limp, I saw two images: myself stuck underneath a roundabout, and Grandad and Grandma holding my hand.

Coughing and spluttering, gasping and struggling for breath, I heard Donald's voice shouting my name, then felt him wrapping a towel around my shivering body. I opened my eyes and stared at him. Slowly, everything returned to normal. By now, Donald was sitting with his head slumped forward on his knees. I sat beside him and held his hand. We sat there silently for some time.

'Donald, I don't want to swim in the sea again. Will you stay with me on the Golden Mile?'

'Listen, Alan. I should have been more careful. Look how big and powerful the sea is. You nearly drowned.'

I looked at the sea for the first time since Donald had pulled me out. I shivered again.

'Listen, Alan.' Donald was visibly shaking. 'Don't tell Grandma and Grandad. I told them I'd look after you.' He suddenly burst into tears.

'Donald, I won't speak a word. We can swim any time but we can't always go on the Golden Mile, can we? If Grandma asks why we aren't going for a swim, I'll just say I'd rather go on the Golden Mile.'

My promise and solution seemed to inspire confidence.

'Right, Alan. Let's get dried properly, get changed, and make our way back to the guest house. You're looking better now. How do you feel?'

'OK.'

It was a wonderful feeling to say OK, and it was a wonderful relief to cross over that busy road back to the Golden Mile. However, we didn't dawdle. We made our way very quickly to the guest house. Grandma was surprised but pleased to see us back earlier than half past eight. It was difficult for me to keep control of myself when I saw my grandparents, especially now they were "all poshed up".

'My, you two look all fresh and clean. Have you enjoyed yourselves?'

'It was great, Grandma, but we decided to come back early because the sea air makes you tired, and we're very tired tonight.' I had heard her say these words about the sea air making you tired several times already, so felt sure she wouldn't disagree with me. In fact, she looked even more pleased.

'It certainly does, Alan. I said the same thing to your grandad when we were walking home for our tea.'

'It might have made you tired, but that sea air's made me thirsty.' Grandad was losing interest.

'Well, Alan, go on, have a good wash, clean your teeth and off to bed. I think your grandad's ready to go downstairs. I hope you've enjoyed your first day in Blackpool. Tomorrow we'll go on the beach when the tide's out, and you can paddle your feet in the sea.'

The following morning, while Donald and I ate our breakfast very quietly, the conversation seemed to surround the surprising speed at which all the guests had "settled into t'digs" and the importance of the sun shining all week so "we can all go back to work looking browned off".

On returning to our rooms, Grandad immediately slumped into his armchair – he had already claimed it for the duration of the holiday – and lit his pipe, looking very contented.

'Eee, this is the life. Nowt to do and all day to do it in.'

Nobody answered him. Grandma was her busy self, instantly occupied on arrival in the room and insisting, 'Nothing's changed. We mustn't start being slovenly just because we're on our holidays.'

Donald and I were still unusually quiet. We must both have looked at a loose end.

'What's wrong with you two? You can't go on the Golden Mile looking like that,' said Grandma, sounding happy and carefree.

'Can I go to that corner shop and get Grandad a morning paper?'

Something must have clicked in my brain, warning me of the dangers of Grandma's questions.

'Good idea, lad. Why didn't I think of that?' Grandad now looked pleased as well as contented.

Still feeling the effects of shock, I wasn't coping very well. It shouldn't have been difficult to keep last night's near-drowning experience a secret from my grandparents, but, seeing them looking much more relaxed and happier than I ever remembered, it wasn't easy. If they discovered the secret, their holiday would be spoiled.

But on my return to the rooms with Grandad's paper, Donald came to my rescue.

'Grandma, can me and Alan go and have a look 'round the Golden Mile? I'll hold his hand, and we'll be back here in good time for dinner.' He sounded his normal calm self.

'We won't cross that – '

'Keep quiet, Alan,' interrupted Grandma. 'Let me think.'

I picked up a comic and pretended to read, forcing my eyes to look at it, in case she questioned the previous night's events. The slightest eye contact might have triggered a flood of questions.

After what seemed an age, probably about five minutes, with Grandad reading and puffing and Grandma tidying and dusting, the silence was broken.

'Well, we were very pleased with you both last night. I wasn't sure about that dangerous road, and then the thought of you in that sea. I'm glad you didn't do anything daft like drowning yourselves. Your grandad's face lit up when you came through that door. All the time he was getting poshed up, he kept complaining about how late you'd be. Right, keep together and be back here half an hour before dinner so you can go downstairs all cleaned up. And don't cross that busy road.'

'Oh, thanks, Grandma!'

Donald sounded excited, but I felt relief. Being away from my grandparents would give me a longer time to come to terms with the sea escapade.

'Another thing, don't take any of your spending money with you. Everybody's happy and smiling, but they're much happier when they're taking all your money.'

'Your grandad's right. You could waste all your spending money just on them fortune tellers – they'll be waiting to empty your pockets while they're telling you that you'll be rich.'

It seemed she was talking from previous experience; it was best to avoid any irritating questions.

'Right, Grandma.' I didn't ask when I would be given permission to "waste" my spending money.

So that Sunday morning, Donald and I strolled hand in hand along the Golden Mile. We just walked aimlessly, not taking in any of the sights on show, but it gradually helped me to settle; we reached the guest house in good time for dinner, and by then, I had more or less returned to my normal self, no longer holding Donald's hand, and beginning to look forward to all the activities the holiday would offer.

In the afternoon, we went onto the beach. Our two main pastimes were building sandcastles to knock down and burying each other up to our heads in the sand. It was fun, but the closeness of the sea still troubled me.

I didn't go into the water. Not for a paddle, not even to fill my bucket to make a moat around my sandcastle. Donald, on the other hand, went in happily, playing and swimming with the other children. He had obviously been very upset at the near disaster, but he wasn't the one who had nearly drowned; his main concern had been keeping the incident a secret from Grandma. This meant that all that sunny Sunday afternoon I played happily, but stayed very close to my grandma. She was glad about this, as Grandad had disappeared to play bowls. Now she could relax and enjoy the warm sunshine. I had never seen her sitting and resting like this. She didn't ask me why I wasn't going in the sea. In fact, she hardly spoke.

'Alan, if you move away from my deckchair to go and play in the sea, please tell me, even if you think I'm asleep.'

'All right, Grandma. I hope you get nice and sunburnt. What if Grandad comes back?'

'Tell him not to disturb me. He'll only be talking non-stop about how he nearly won his game of bowls. He can moan about that tonight when we're having a drink downstairs.'

'All right, Grandma.'

So the afternoon continued calmly and uneventfully. I saw my grandad approaching and ran to him. 'Don't waken Grandma. She said you can tell her about how you nearly won when you go downstairs tonight.'

'Listen, lad, between me and you, I did win – so put that in your pipe and smoke it! But don't tell your grandma; it's between me and you.'

'OK, Grandad.' I waited to be corrected, but nothing happened. From that moment, I felt it was all right to say OK anywhere in the world, if my grandma couldn't hear me.

After tea, Grandma, with growing confidence in Donald's responsibility, gave us leave to stroll on the Golden Mile with money in our pockets to spend, but with clear instructions to be back in the guest house for half past eight.

'Donald, I was a bit worried when you went out last night, but I didn't need to be. You were both very good, and when we went downstairs, we had a lovely time. This is a wonderful holiday.'

So, once again we left the guest house, this time without our suitcases. Neither of us found it necessary to hold hands, but even so I stayed close to Donald, especially as we approached the Golden Mile. The bumping, jostling and general jockeying for position was clearly common practice, making me more aware of the importance of keeping him in close sight.

Up to this point, everything had been too much to take in, but now I was settling down; I had been on the Golden Mile, or at least on the fringe of it, several times, but it was still unbelievable. It was a hubbub of noisy, clamorous confusion, with little pockets of flashing coloured lights. I was mesmerised. My grandma was right. People of all sorts, some with high-pitched, squeaky voices, some with loud sergeant-major booming shouts, were tempting happy but vulnerable holidaymakers to part with their hard-earned and religiously-saved spending money.

'Who cares about money? If you're having a good time, it's worth it.'

'Spend your money and have some fun – you deserve it!'

'First to twenty-one wins a prize!' These words were being repeated by a jovial, sunburnt man. The game was to roll a wooden ball, half the size of a tennis ball, into one of three holes at the top of a bagatelle table, each hole having a different points value. When the ball went into a hole, it would trigger a moving finger on a clock face, numbered 1 to 21, at the top of each table. After it had gone through the hole, the ball would reappear at the bottom of the table to be rolled again.

'First to twenty-one wins a prize, sixpence a game.'

I looked at the massive array of prizes, each one displaying the number of wins needed, and made up my mind that here, on this part of the Golden Mile, I would spend all my money.

'Donald, I want to spend all my money on this game.'

'Are you sure, Alan?' Donald seemed taken aback. 'Why don't you save some?'

'Grandma gave it to me to spend.' I had made a decision. My grandma had given me half-a-crown to spend how I liked, and "first to twenty-one" was it.

'Anyway, I've picked out a prize if I win. I want to try to win you a tennis set. Can you see it, on the second shelf? Two tennis racquets and two tennis balls. It's two wins.'

'Oh, Alan, that would be great.' Donald, his cautious attitude vanishing, was suddenly infected with great enthusiasm.

I had half-a-crown to spend that day, which gave me five games and five chances. I sat down and paid my money. While the man with the sunburnt face was collecting money from other hopeful contestants, those who had paid were allowed to practise. Immediately, I found the knack of rolling the ball into the hole worth three points, the largest value. That night, I played five games and won five games. It was wonderful; the scowling faces of the other players didn't bother me at all. When we returned to the guest house, Donald had a tennis racquet and I had a cricket set, as well as one ticket towards my next prize. By the end of the week, Grandad had a real leather tobacco pouch and Grandma had a brass poker and stand and a brass coal scuttle.

One day during this wonderful week, we were taken to the Tower Zoo. I can still see the tiger and the lion padding up and down their glass-fronted cages. They looked sad and lonely, but completely fearless and frighteningly untouchable. The monkeys, too, looked dangerous, but within the confines of their cage, they just seemed comical, especially when performing their foolish, non-stop acrobatics, accompanied by their silly chattering and mimicry.

Every experience was new, and, apart from the alarming sea episode, all interesting and often exciting. However, the one incident I think back to more than any other would, for most people, seem the most innocuous. During our visit to the Tower, my grandparents, Grandma in particular, decided to visit the Tower Ballroom. Everyone was talking about the famous Reginald Dixon, though he was not there; his replacement was playing the favourite tunes of the day and of days gone by. Donald and I were plonked down at the edge of the ballroom, with the strictest orders to watch quietly and enjoy the music. But then, I was fascinated to see my grandparents dancing together around the ballroom. It was such an unexpected sight, and nothing, except perhaps an escaping lion or tiger, could have dragged my eyes from it.

Another day was reserved for Madame Tussauds. It seemed hard to believe that those figures were not alive. I stared intensely into their eyes and waited expectantly for some movement. I became so frightened going through the murderers section that I closed my eyes and clung on tightly to Grandad's jacket. Despite this, I asked my grandma if we could stay in the building after the lights had been switched off so that we might be able to find out which of them were alive.

Strange as it may seem, the visit to the Pleasure Beach turned out to be the least fun. We had walked the entire length of the Golden Mile and more to reach it. I had been expecting some kind of special sand, and had linked the word "pleasure" to Grandad's earlier comment, 'That's when the fun and games start.' For some reason, nothing would tempt me to have a go on the Waltzer, the Dodgems, the Big Wheel, the Ghost Train or the Big Dipper. In fact, I would have been content to spend my time at the Pleasure Beach entrance, watching the Laughing Clown. However, in taking in the sights and sounds, it was obvious that for most people the Pleasure Beach was the place for fun and games.

Crazy golf and putting were fun, with Grandma sitting on a bench enjoying the scene while I tried, unsuccessfully, to beat Grandad and Donald. We enjoyed a horse and carriage ride up and down the Golden Mile, and took an open-top tram from the Pleasure Beach along the entire sea front before returning to the Central Pier. Grandad played bowls every day and Grandma spent time in the "big shops". The tennis racquets and cricket set were both well used; Donald and I played every day, usually when Grandma was in those big shops. The owners of the guest house had directed us to some nearby open grassland which my grandma had passed as a safe place to play. So, every day of our holiday was simply wonderful.

But, as my grandma would say, all good things come to an end.

'Well, lad, it's back to carrying th'owd kitbag, but this time it's going home. Polly, first thing to do when we get home is put that kettle on; let's have a proper cup of tea.'

'Have you not had a good time, Grandad? You seem glad to be going.' I was surprised by his cheery attitude.

'I've had a good time, lad, but I want to get back to my tomatoes. They'd better all not be shrivelled up.'

'Come on, Alan, don't get your grandad talking about tomatoes or we'll be here for another week. Have you got your suitcase packed?'

'Yes, Grandma.'

'Have you tied your bucket and spade on?'

'Yes, Grandma.'

She sounded impatient, and slightly flustered, but suddenly became kind and gentle.

'Alan, are you sure you can carry my brass coal scuttle as well?'

'Yes, Grandma, it's not heavy; there's no coal in it.'

Grandad chuckled at my cheeky answer. She was too concerned, though, with leaving the rooms spick and span, to spend time chastising me; even so, I felt very brave.

Eventually, we were ready to go to the station, and for the final time, sadly, we departed from the guest house. The walk to the station was the same as before, Grandad carrying our large suitcase on his shoulder, Grandma with her handbag and shopping basket, me with my suitcase and its tied-on bucket, spade and brass coal scuttle, and Donald with his tennis racquets. This time, though, Donald didn't try to trip me; I think we all felt gloomy.

This feeling, especially for me, evaporated when we entered the station. That electrifying hubbub of activity, the busy porters, the sunburnt holidaymakers, the people waving goodbye, the trains hissing, gasping and complaining, all accompanied by the loudspeakers ringing around the platforms; all this was more than enough to dispel my gloom and return me to a trance-like state.

We were allowed to walk along to see the magnificent steam engine. Its awesome power seemed to radiate; close up to it, I felt trapped, completely ensnared by its frightening beauty. The regular, short bursts of steam revealed its impatience to start the homeward journey, a journey back from the edge of the world to the centre of the earth.

The return journey had a familiar feel. Once again, a third class compartment; once again, the leather window strap, but now I was waving goodbye to the sad-looking platform people. The porters had disappeared.

The conversation in that crammed compartment consisted of two distinct topics in two distinct halves. The discussion during the first half of the journey was based entirely on the week's experiences, shared like ours between the sea and beach, the Golden Mile, the Tower and the Pleasure Beach. Then the conversation switched to the more mundane matters that lay ahead. There was no moaning or complaining, though; the general tone was of light banter and good humour.

We eventually arrived at our station, so for the final time, I expertly released the leather window strap. This station was familiar, the busy porters, the waiting people looking relieved and the echoing loudspeakers. Grandma allowed us the last close-up view of the steaming engine until, hissing and complaining, it shunted its way down the platform, leaving us momentarily invisible in smoke and steam. Then, with Grandad still refusing help to carry the 'lighter than mi kitbag' suitcase, we slowly made our way to the bus stop for the bus that would take us to our field.

'Eee, it's good to be home,' exclaimed Grandad as we crossed the field.

'Polly, put kettle on as soon as we get in, while I go and check my tomatoes.'

I thought Grandma would be too busy to make a pot of tea. On the train home, she had made it plain to all and sundry that she was going home to a "list full of jobs". But surprisingly, the tea was made, and very quickly, we were all sat together around the table.

'Eee, this is a gradely cup of tea. It's worth coming home to, but seeing my tomatoes are all right makes it even better.' Grandad was happy.

'Well, Alan, did you enjoy your holiday?' Grandma sounded content too.

'Yes, Grandma. Every day was wonderful.'

'What did you like best of all?'

'I liked everything. I've got a list full of the exciting things we did.' The mention of a list didn't seem to irritate her; she just sat happily drinking her tea. Then she suddenly spoke.

'I'm glad you mentioned a list, Alan. When we've finished our tea, I'll write one and you can go to Holmes' shop. We're not going back to the guest house for our tea. I'll have to make it.'

This was my grandma trying to be funny, but it was clear to me that our wonderful holiday was at an end.

# My Other Grandad

After about two years of living with my grandparents, I started to go on regular Sunday visits to another aged parent, my father's father. This was a definite "my brother and I" situation. We went to see our other grandad once a month, sometimes twice, in the early Sunday afternoon. The timetable was Sunday School in the morning, walk home, dinner; then, depending on the state of the weather, it was one of two plans. If the weather was fine, we walked through the park and out the other end, through the large ornamental main gates. We called them the "American Gates" because it was through here that the Americans flocked in, most holding hands with a woman.

After these gates, we made our way past the formidable-looking building where "all the clever people go". Donald told me this was the grammar school. At the side of it, was a very large area of grassland surrounded by a dense hedge. On one Saturday trip into town, I was fascinated to see, through a gap in the hedge, people dressed in white playing cricket. I had never seen real cricket; it didn't look like the game we played on our field.

Anyway, on our Sunday visits we had to cross the town centre, taking a short cut through the main area of shops; the "little arcade" and the "big arcade" saved us from having to walk all the way around. They ran parallel to each other about fifty yards apart. If they were both open, Donald went through one and I went through the other to see who won. Once, I doubled back and followed behind him, hiding near the top in a shop alcove. He searched for me for about ten minutes before I revealed my whereabouts.

'Where have you been? I've been looking all over the place for you!'

Donald looked and sounded very relieved to see me.

'Hiding from you. I knew you wouldn't spot me.'

'You stupid thing. I was really worried. I thought you'd got lost. What would Grandma say if I told her that? Soon as I get home I'm telling her.' Donald was very angry and I could see he meant it.

'I'm sorry, Donald. It was only meant to be a game. Listen, if I give you my silver threepenny bit, will you not tell Grandma?'

'Right, well, stay with me in town and don't be so stupid.'

It was my turn to feel relieved.

So, on that day, when our other grandad gave us our usual silver threepenny bit, Donald went home with two.

After the short cut, we crossed a very busy main road, with cars and buses coming from all directions. The road seemed to be as wide as four roads put together, so I was really glad Donald was there. I always felt safe with him. Then, after crossing this wide road, we turned down a side street to a bus stop that would take us to our other grandad's.

The other plan was much simpler. If the weather was poor we caught a bus to town and made our way down the side street, with no arcades to cut through, to the bus stop, then onto the bus and straight upstairs with the smokers. It wasn't the smokers that attracted me, it was the feeling of being on top of the world.

I would have been lost without my brother on these trips. Once, however, we had fallen out and he refused to sit with me. I went upstairs and he stayed downstairs. It would be difficult for me when it came to getting off the bus at the right stop. I began to worry. What if Donald got off the bus without letting me know? Then he would be laughing at me from the pavement, waiting for me to walk all the way back from the next stop.

The "mirror technique" came to my rescue. I had noticed it before, but never tested it out. The convex mirror, fastened strategically on the stairwell halfway down the stairs, was for the conductress to see from upstairs if people were waiting to leave the bus. She could then ring the bell – "press once for stop". So on the day we had the disagreement, I watched for Donald. Once he appeared in the mirror, I clattered triumphantly down the stairs, as if I really knew the way. He pretended he wasn't bothered.

One day, an inspector came up the stairs. Normally, I kept my ticket, and pushed it into the gaping "Used Tickets" letterbox when I got off. Sometimes I rolled and rolled my ticket between my fingers and thumbs into the thinnest cigarette shape. Today was a roll-up day. But after a while, interest in the roll-up waned and the ticket was forgotten. Being on the front seat, I probably turned my attention to driving the bus. When the inspector came up the stairs, I knew I had lost my ticket. It wasn't in my hand, it wasn't in my pocket and it wasn't on the seat.

'Tickets, please.'

The inspector moved down the aisle towards the front of the bus.

'Tickets, please.'

He loomed over me and held out his hand.

'I've lost it. It must be on the floor somewhere.'

'There's a place for used tickets, and it isn't on the floor. Find your ticket or you'll have to pay for another one.'

He walked back along the aisle and disappeared down the stairs. I looked down; the floor was covered in used tickets.

I went down the stairs.

'I'm sorry, I can't find my ticket. There's too many other used tickets on the floor.'

'Listen carefully,' he said. 'The bus conductress insists you've paid, so I'm not going to charge you for another ticket. But in future, keep hold of your ticket, and when you leave the bus, put it in the used tickets letterbox. You probably never even knew it existed. Go on, get off the bus, and be more careful in future.'

These are the kinds of things that happened on the journeys to our other grandad's. Loitering in the park or around the big shop windows, was our most common activity. When one of us thought of the waiting silver threepenny bit, the loitering would stop.

My other grandad lived in a public house. The two front rooms were dark and gloomy, with a rank smell, a mixture of ale and smoke from cigarettes and pipes.

Nevertheless, we spent a lot of time on our Sunday afternoons in those rooms. Pressing the buttons on the wall behind the long brown leather seats was always good fun. These buttons were used by customers to order drinks, and we expected a drink of dandelion and burdock every time we pressed one. On Sunday afternoons the pub was closed, so we had the rooms to ourselves, and could play dominoes, cards and darts, games that were not available at Grandma's house. Darts was a struggle, even to hit the dartboard.

We were restricted to these rooms. Grandad's living quarters were upstairs, but for some unknown reason, we were not allowed to climb those stairs.

The house was just off the main road, reached by crossing a bridge over a stream. Donald and I had many hours of fun just throwing corks of various sizes, obtained from a big crate in the corner of one of the front rooms, into the stream and watching them disappearing under the bridge, to emerge triumphant on the other side. To look over the bridge we had to climb onto the top of a stone wall, then peer down into the stream, waiting excitedly for the corks. If mine was first, Donald would sulk and try to push me into the stream; luckily he never managed this, but occasionally, he would push me back onto the bridge, often making me cry. It was all good fun.

The most important fun was reserved for the back of the pub. The back door opened onto a partly paved, partly cobbled, partly cindery square courtyard, with six stables around the edges. Alas, the horses were gone, and now the stables were used for different purposes, two of them for the storage of bowls, the bowling green being through an open entrance to one side of the courtyard. The gates taking you to the front of the house were never opened. On reflection, those closed gates saved me a lot of trouble.

The bowling green was one of our favourite places. The bowls were too heavy for me, so Grandad let me play with the smaller jack. I tried to bowl it from corner to corner without it falling into the gully. Sometimes, I took lots of jacks from the stables and tried to bowl them across the green so that they all touched each other. I once had seven of them very close together on the green – but twenty-three much closer together in the gully.

Surrounding the bowling green, which was completely enclosed apart from the entrance, were a number of benches similar to those in the park. But these seats, unlike those in the park, crammed with Americans and their girlfriends, were always empty. I often sat and watched Donald play, using a full-sized bowl. He denied it, but it was a struggle for him. I laughed at him and taunted him, especially when a bowl slipped out of his hand to trickle and stop just a few feet away from him.

Behind the seats, more or less all the way around the bowling green, were trees and dense shrubbery. We were allowed to climb the trees, and we could also run and hide and generally have fun in the bushes. The only restriction, and we were both aware of it, was, 'Mind your best suits,' usually the last warning words issued by Grandma at the start of each pub visit. In the summer, we spent all our time in those trees.

One fine Sunday afternoon, we were playing there when Grandad suddenly appeared. This was unusual.

'Come here, you two. I want to show you something.' Thankfully, he didn't sound annoyed.

We instantly stopped playing and obediently walked towards him. Whenever I was standing directly in front of my other grandad, I felt uneasy and sometimes frightened. He was a tall, heavily-built man whose voice sounded loud and harsh, never gentle and kind. It seemed to me that, in the normal state of affairs, he was bad-tempered.

'Follow me.'

We followed quietly behind him as he moved awkwardly into a dense part of the shrubbery.

'Right, look in there.' His voice sounded slightly excited as he directed his gaze towards the darkness.

Donald was the first to become accustomed to the change from light to dark. 'It's a bird's nest,' he said triumphantly, probably half-expecting some praise, but if there was any forthcoming from Grandad, my reaction was sufficient to quell it.

'Let me see it. Please show me,' I said excitedly.

Donald too was unable to contain his excitement. He clambered into a position from where he could look directly into the bird's nest. Unexpectedly, I was lifted by Grandad into a similar position. Resting comfortably in the bottom of a cup-shaped nest were five light-greenish-blue, slightly mottled blackbird's eggs. I was thrilled at the sight.

'I'll give you one each to take home. If you keep them warm they'll hatch in a few weeks. Then you can feed them and make them tame.'

I couldn't believe what was happening, but that day, as promised, we set off on our journey home with our eggs wrapped in cotton wool.

'Hold the egg in your hand; keep your hand closed gently.'

Grandad's advice was heeded, up to a point. On the journey home, though, it was very difficult to keep my balance when climbing the stairs of the moving bus, holding the egg in one hand and the handrail in the other.

Having arrived safely in town, I decided the next bus ride would be a downstairs journey. Unluckily, there was, as Grandma would say, a queue a mile long. We eventually got on the bus; Donald went upstairs and I followed the people into the downstairs section, helped by the conductress's cheery command, 'Move along, please, move to the front.'

To my dismay, I had to stand up; those with seats looked smug and distinctly pleased with themselves. Normally, if I was sitting down and "standing-room only" came along, I gave up my seat willingly, but not today. If someone left his seat, I would be first to take his place. Nobody moved, and as the journey unfolded, I realised the continuous swaying, bumping, lurching and sudden jolting that came with stopping and starting all meant one thing, the need to hold onto the rail with both hands. So I put the egg, still wrapped in cotton wool, into the side pocket of my best suit. At the next bump and jostle, I knew the egg had been broken.

I experienced a mixture of emotions, wondering what state my suit was in and how my grandma would react. Donald would taunt me and show off with his blackbird's egg. Most of all I wanted to cry, but bravely held back the tears until we got off the bus.

A lady from a nearby street who knew Grandma was walking past. Seeing me crying, she stopped, looking concerned.

'What's wrong, Alan? Have you hurt yourself?'

'No, it's my bird's egg and my best suit pocket,' I wailed.

'What do you mean?'

'Grandad gave me a bird's egg so I could bring up a tame blackbird, but it's broken in my pocket. Grandma's going to smack me.'

'It's wrapped up in cotton wool, like mine,' said Donald, showing the lady his unbroken egg.

‘Let me have a look, Alan,’ she said coaxingly, gently removing the small ball of cotton wool from my pocket. ‘Well, you’ve been very lucky. This cotton wool has soaked up all the mess. I’ll just make sure.’

She took out a clean handkerchief from her bag and vigorously wiped the inside lining of my pocket.

‘See, Alan, there’s no mess on my handkerchief. You won’t get smacked, so you can stop worrying.’

On the way across our field, Donald didn’t taunt me; in fact, he suggested, that we should both look after his blackbird’s egg.

However, it all proved in vain. There was no little fledgling to feed or tame; we were left just with an addled egg.

In the winter time, outdoor activities were scarcer, and when one came along, we welcomed it. On one splendid day, the snow was lying very deep, so when we arrived at our grandad’s, it was straight out to play. We couldn’t see a footprint on the bowling green, only bird tracks, which I immediately started to follow. Donald and I made a snowman each, then together we made a big one. We threw snowballs at all of them, we threw snowballs at the birds watching in the trees, and we threw snowballs at each other.

So it was that, at our other grandad’s, Donald and I spent most of the time in each other’s company. But there were times when we drifted apart and occupied ourselves in individual interests. On that snowy, wintry day, playing games on the bowling green, that was exactly what happened.

I wandered into the courtyard and made my way towards the pig. One of the old stables had been turned into a pigsty. I opened the stable door and stepped onto the thick layer of straw that covered the stone floor. Facing me was the pigsty, a wooden, horizontally-railed enclosure. I sat on the top rail dangling my feet, as usual facing into the sty. It was a big pig, and my grandad said, it would bite me if I wasn’t careful, so I always kept my eye on that pig.

Sometimes, Grandad gave me the silver threepenny bit sooner rather than later. Today was a sooner day, and I sat on the top rail of the pigsty inspecting it. After the inspection, I began tossing it into the air to guess heads or tails, at least I did until the silver threepenny bit inevitably dropped into the pigsty. Now the pig’s squeals and grunts stopped being funny; they suddenly sounded frightening. My shiny threepenny bit was lying on top of thick mud, tantalisingly just out of reach of my straining hand. I felt, though, it was reachable if I opened the gate.

I opened the gate. The pig seemed to lose control, squealing, grunting and banging its heavy body against the rails, and it was so fast. The pig streaked through the opening, sending me flying onto the thick straw and mud, disappearing onto the bowling green; that was the last time I saw it for the next few months.

In the commotion before its escape, my silver threepenny bit had sunk forever into the mud, though I managed a quick but fruitless look for it before Donald came racing across the courtyard shouting for Grandad.

'Grandad, the pig's racing on the bowling green!'

When my grandad came into the courtyard, in his large overcoat and flat cap, he was carrying a long pole. I thought he was going to hit me with that big stick, but thankfully, it was only to guide the pig back into the sty.

'You two, inside, quick!' He looked furious.

We both ran into the front room, never looking back. All the time we were in that room, Donald was complaining.

'Why could I not see Grandad catch the pig? I never let it out. I even told him it was running on the bowling green. If I hadn't told him, he would never have known. I think he should have let me watch him catch the pig. I'm fed up. Anyway, how did it get out of the pigsty?'

'My silver threepenny bit fell into the mud, and I opened the door to get it.'

'Well, that's stupid.'

'Well, what would you have done?'

'I wouldn't have been daft enough to drop my silver threepenny bit into the mud. See, I've still got mine.'

'I don't need to see it. I've seen a silver threepenny bit before.' I was fed up now.

Just then, Grandad came into the room.

'I've never seen anything so daft. If that bowling green's been damaged, you two are in trouble. Get your coats on quick.' He turned to Donald. 'Right, you, when you get home, give this letter to your grandma. Get going, there's a bus due.'

We waited for what seemed ages for a bus; it was probably about ten minutes.

'I wish the bus would come before he finds out the bowling green's damaged,' said Donald.

'How do you know that it's damaged?'

'Because it's a big, fat, heavy pig. Listen, Alan, I want to know what's in this letter. I shouldn't get blamed for this. Whatever's in this letter, Grandma will believe.'

'What do you think we should do?'

'We'll have to steam it open.'

'Will you do it, Donald? You're older than me.'

'All right.'

The opportunity arrived the following day after school, with Grandad at work and Grandma at Mrs Whitaker's, our neighbour three doors down, who had been ill.

'Quick, Alan, light the gas. I hope it doesn't run out.'

It seemed to take ages to boil, but finally steam spouted out of the kettle.

Donald held the corner of the envelope as he moved it through the steam.

'Right, it's steaming open,' said Donald.

There was one piece of paper inside the envelope.

He read the note aloud. It was brief. What annoyed him, but pleased me, was that the note incriminated him in the incident.

'These children let my pig escape onto the bowling green,' it said. The second sentence was just as brief. 'If they do anything silly like this again, don't send them anymore.'

Because Donald was being blamed, he decided, and I readily agreed, that we should throw the letter onto the fire. He would do it and make sure it burned. I can still see him poking the letter until it was ash. I didn't argue. If it ever came to light, I would be able to say that it wasn't me who threw it onto the fire. I'm pleased to say that it never did.

# Games to Play

Much of my early life was spent in the park. In the summertime, it was beautiful. The "Keep off the Grass" areas looked magnificent, with wide borders of glorious rainbow-coloured flowers. The play areas were mainly open grassland; the one I liked best, had swings and roundabouts. I often used to watch Grandad happily playing bowls, occasionally waving to me. A lot of the men playing with him had only one arm or one leg; in fact, I would sometimes sit on one of the seats next to men who had no legs. They all seemed to know Grandad, and strangely, they all seemed to know me.

'Eee, Alan, your grandad's playing well today.'

'Well, lad, you can tell your grandad, I think he's looking well.'

'I hope you're a good lad for your grandad.'

I always liked to sit watching my grandad play bowls.

Sometimes, when he had three pence to spare, he would give me a game of putting. The putting green lay between the bowling greens and tennis courts. Putting with Grandad meant playing to the rules. He used to say some wise words: 'If you cheat, you only cheat yourself', 'It's better to have lost while trying your best rather than to have won by cheating'.

When we played on the putting green, Grandad wasn't trying to beat me; he was trying to achieve a hole in one. Whenever he got a hole in one, he likened the golf ball to a grenade, destroying the enemy's machine-gun position. If he struggled to get that grenade into the hole, our casualty list would grow; the number of putts equated to the number of casualties. I suppose it comes down to inferior coordination and other things, but I always had a great number of casualties, and never destroyed a machine gun.

In winter, we used to slide on the bandstand. Regularly, there would be thirty or forty children making slides; I don't know if we were officially allowed to do this, or whether it was just by sheer weight of numbers, with the park keeper turning a blind eye. Every icy spell, if it happened on a weekend, would find five or six groups of children making five or six long slides. We all knew each other; nobody seemed to fall out, but we all knew which group to join. They were groups rather than gangs, because it was only on occasions, like the icy weekends, we would gather together.

The bandstand was on a raised platform. Around it was a circular area, about twenty yards wide; in the summertime, this was prime seating for spectators to enjoy the wonderful bands that played most Sundays. It was on this spectator area that the slides were made. We ran along the grass and started to slide the moment our feet touched the tarmac, part of the increasing excitement being the gradual lengthening of the slippery surface. There were at least eight starting and finishing points, many slides crossing each other.

When the slides were at their fastest, we might be careering down at lightning speed just as a member of a different group was approaching the crossroads. This was always excellent fun, with the most daring of us trying to time our slides to just miss each other. Not satisfied with this excitement, we tried other techniques. Running at a fair speed onto the slide enabled you to turn your back towards the fast approaching danger; if you looked to the front, you had failed. Backwards was difficult because you couldn't help speeding up, and finding yourself hurtling along, not seeing where you were going, hoping that you would crash safely into the grass verge. We also closed our eyes, crouched down or glided on one leg; all of these skills needed balance at speed.

The nearest summer activity to these "near misses" and occasional "direct hits" was Grandad's sport of bowls. The men's bowls crossed from all directions but always seemed to miss each other. I know it isn't very sporting, and he never knew, but I would close my eyes and wish everybody's bowls would collide – except my grandad's.

Most of the time, I was part of a group. Cricket in the summer, football in the winter – 'Never the twain shall meet.' These games were fixtures, but we also enjoyed hopscotch, roller-skating and marbles when the craze took hold.

Two games that came top of my list were making lead pellets for catapults and using cartridge cases for arrows. No one ever thought about these pellets; it was always an integral part of our summer activity. It was like making a cake; the required ingredients were a pan, dry sticks, paper, matches and damp sand. And lead, of course. We fixed up pieces of wood into a square shape, and then packed in the sand; by pushing a finger into it, we made numerous small holes. The lead, and there always seemed plenty of old piping thrown away, was collected from hedgerows and the railway banking. We always had a supply of knives and saws made from nails and screws with the aid of a "Jubilee" or a "Patriot", those helpful trains. If no one had a jackknife, we used these sharp implements to cut the lead into smaller pieces. These went into the pan, the fire was set going, the lead melted and carefully poured into the sand holes. The result was small, reasonably round pellets for our catapults. We always made a large supply of ammunition.

Making these pellets was, in itself, an enjoyable pastime, but the reward was even better. I can't remember ever using our catapults for anything more dangerous than lining up tin cans along the railway embankment wall and firing lead pellets from various distances. It was always a victorious feeling to hit a tin with one of these home-made pellets. Whenever a train came by, maybe because we were busy checking its number in our books, nobody fired their catapults until the train had passed the target area.

The bullet cartridges, using the pointed end, were fitted onto lengths of cane dowelling varying between twelve and eighteen inches in length. The cane had to be pared down so that it fitted snugly into the cartridge case, which was between one and two inches long. The opposite end of the arrow was the most difficult. The success of the arrow was down to the cardboard flights slotted into carefully-made cross slits. If you were lucky, your flights ended up with some of the dowel jutting out. This enabled you to bind cotton around the top of the dowel so that the flights were firmly held. With the arrow ready, all that was needed was a length of string with a knot in one end. Loop the string around the arrow and over the knot, just below the flights; run the string down the arrow, wrapping the surplus string around your hand. Holding the arrow and string at the bullet end, throw the arrow as if you were throwing a cricket ball, retaining hold of the string. The arrow is released, and the result is marvellous. When successful, my arrow went twice as high and twice as far as I could ever throw a cricket ball. I used to play on my own with my arrow and string for hours on end.

In the winter, my brother and I played together more. We were not allowed out at night; there was no street lighting in our field, and on moonless nights, it was very dark. We played snakes and ladders, Ludo, blow football, battleships and, towards the end of those four years, cards and dominoes. Competition was fierce, but Donald usually won. Our main pastime was reading from cover to cover the fortnightly comics which were swapped around among all the boys.

Grandma took advantage of these winter months, and I seemed to be involved in more household chores than in the summer. One of these was "The Recitations", which usually fitted in with the visits of relatives; I performed this chore unwillingly.

'Right, Alan, after our tea, when we're all sat down, I want everybody to see how clever you are.'

I knew what was coming, so I voiced my reluctance weakly. 'But Grandma, they've heard me before.'

'That doesn't matter, Alan. Good things come in small parcels.'

This stumped me. 'What do you mean, Grandma?'

'Alan, you're like a little precious parcel. When you open it, it fills you with delight and pleasure, and when you do your recitations, you make everybody smile. Everybody is happy.'

I didn't dare show my aversion by mentioning the incidental fact that I wouldn't be smiling; I wouldn't be happy.

These recitations would always be part of the after-tea activities; when everybody had settled down, I would become the centre of attraction.

'Come on, Alan, let's hear them again. I've never heard anybody else saying them.' This was the first relative.

'You know, neither have I. I think there's only Alan in the whole world who knows them.' Another relative.

'Come on then, Alan, take centre stage.' First relative again.

I wasn't sure what "centre stage" meant, but I knew this was my cue to stand up and give my recitation of "Mickey Thumb" and "My Grandfather's Duck Eggs". As long as I live, I don't think I will ever forget the words.

**Mickey Thumb**

As I went walking down Treacle Lane
For half a pound of treacle,
I met my old sweetheart Mickey Thumb.

He said, 'Are you going to the fair tonight?'
I thought a bit and I thought a bit,
Then I said, 'I might as well.'

It was a fair, eee it was a fair,
But nine o'clock came, ten o'clock came,
But no Mickey Thumb turned up.
So I went home.

I hadn't been in the house five minutes
Before a fat chap came to the door.
He said, 'Do you know your old sweetheart Mickey Thumb?'
I said, 'Yes.'
He said, 'Well, he's ill in bed,
And wants to know, will you come and see him?'

I thought a bit and I thought a bit,
Then I said, 'Well, I might as well.'
And he was bad, oh, he was bad.
He said, 'Will you come to my funeral when I die?'
'Well,' I said, 'I might as well.'

Eee, and it was a funeral, it was a funeral.
Some laughed over the grave,
Some cried over the grave,
But I jumped into the grave,
To be with my old sweetheart,
My own Mickey Thumb.

**My Grandfather's Duck Eggs**

One day I was sent to the shop
For my grandfather's duck eggs.
I went in the shop and said,
'Please can I have my grandfather's duck eggs?'
The shopkeeper said, 'I've no bags left.
Where are you going to put them?'
'I know,' I said, 'I'll put one in this pocket
And I'll put one in that pocket.'
So the shopkeeper gave me the duck eggs,
And I put one in this pocket
And I put one in that pocket.
When I got home, my grandma said,
'Why have you not got your grandfather's duck eggs?'
'But I have got them, Grandma.
The shopkeeper had no bags,
So I put one in this pocket,
And I put one in that pocket –
Oh, Grandma, I've broken
My grandfather's duck eggs!'

At the end of each recitation, the audience responded enthusiastically. Occasionally, though, to my horror, they insisted on another performance, especially of "Mickey Thumb", even though sometimes they looked sad.

It didn't stop at visitors. Grandma, usually when we were all darning socks or reading comics, would suddenly say, 'Come on, Alan, let's hear about Mickey Thumb.'

Before the recitations, I was filled with dismay. After them, the feeling was of relief, compounded by the happiness of seeing Grandma's proud and smiling face, and reaping the reward of an extra-large spoonful of malt.

One time we were allowed out in the dark, with strict instructions to stay together, was when we went carol singing. Grandma let us go carol singing starting one week before Christmas. Generally, Donald and I stayed together, but went down separate garden paths so that we could sing at twice as many doors. I have never been able to work out why I didn't mind singing carols, by myself, in an open street, when I wouldn't sing a note in any other situation. Because of the pitch black, we each had a torch to light our way. I could see Donald's torch light going down a garden path, but I couldn't see him. Sometimes, I imagined him to be a ghost; it certainly looked eerie, especially when the mist was swirling.

I have many happy memories of carol singing, but the two most vivid memories aren't among them, although the first one did end well. I had started to sing *Good King Wenceslas* when the door opened and I was invited into the house. I must have looked a pitiful little boy, especially in moments like this, but they didn't show any pity. The man put a shilling – a lot of money – on the table and said, 'Sing.' I sang *Good King Wenceslas* (first verse), *While Shepherds Watched their Flocks by Night* (first verse), *Once in Royal David's City* (first verse), *The First Nowell* (first verse) and *O Come All Ye Faithful* (first verse). Then my lip started to tremble. The lady lifted up the shilling and gave it to me; the man opened the door and said, 'Well done, lad.'

The second vivid memory is sad. When singing a few carols at one house and just finishing off with the usual 'If you haven't got a penny…', I heard the window above the door slide open. My eager anticipation was dampened by a pan, full of freezing water. I went home wet, cold and crying.

It was moments such as this that usually ended up with two of my favourite memories: first, listening to Grandma say, 'Come on, Alan, I'll give you a big spoonful of malt,' and second, listening to Grandad say, 'Eee, thar a rum lad.'

# A Bucketful of Coal

During those happy days being brought up by my grandparents, I learned and remembered a great deal. My grandma had only one way to teach me.

'Right, Alan, come and watch me clean the brass. Watch carefully because it will be one of your jobs.'

'Right, Alan, come and watch me mend your socks. Watch carefully because it will be one of your jobs.'

I did watch carefully, then, in her presence, I would do the job. One of the earliest ones was to polish the furniture; I had a fast introduction to her teaching methods.

'Well, Alan, you've watched me. Now this week, let me see how you manage.'

She would polish once a week, but the strange thing was that there was no before and after difference – the furniture was always gleaming. She was especially proud of her living room table top and her long sideboard top; they were like glass, without even a fingerprint or smudge.

'All right, Grandma, can I stand on the chair to polish the table top?'

'Yes, but be careful. And don't forget about the legs.'

'Yes, Grandma.'

'Right, I'll leave you to it. I'm just taking these tomatoes to Mrs Whittaker's. When I get back, if you've done a good job, you can go out to play for a while.'

'Oh, thanks, Grandma.'

Thoughts of going out to play always made me happy, and often would set me dreaming of adventure. In addition, it seemed to me now that the shining furniture didn't need any improvement, so the Mansion Polish tin remained closed. All that was needed, I thought, was a good dusting.

When Grandma came back from Mrs Whittaker's, I had finished and was waiting to go out to play.

'Right, Grandma, can I go out and play hopscotch now?'

'I've a good mind to send you hopping off to bed. Go and get that polish from the cupboard, and bring a rag and duster.'

I could see something had annoyed her, but was slow to realise what it could be.

'Right, Alan, come here.'

She opened the tin and thrust it into my face.

'Can you smell that polish? That tin has never been opened. Get all this furniture polished properly, and then you get a good wash and clean your teeth. And before you go to bed, let me see if you smell of soap or Mansion polish.'

I knew, now I couldn't deceive my grandma, and from then onwards, I would always try my best. Sometimes I had to muddle through, persevere and improve until I got her nod of approval. I found the jobs difficult or uninteresting to begin with, but eventually began to enjoy them.

For example, cleaning the brasses; I initially classed it as a punishment. Grandma loved her brass; the house was full of the stuff, candlesticks large and small, horse brasses, belt after belt full, clocks, scuttles, poker stands and buckets, in the kitchen, dining room and parlour. Polish, clean off, polishing rag to finish.

I didn't know whether it was because I had to do them or because Grandma loved them, probably a mixture of both, but it didn't seem to take long for my attitude to change; I soon approached brass-cleaning with great gusto and a sense of pride and achievement. I also became skilled at peeling potatoes, turnips and carrots, chopping onions, cauliflower and cabbage, mending socks, using a bobbin, sewing buttons, washing up, and cleaning windows, enjoying them all.

'Alan, you're doing that job very well.'

'Alan, you're becoming an expert at that.'

Grandma's praise always made me feel good, especially with its usual promise of an extra spoonful of malt.

My outside job for Grandma was to go to the local shop, a corner shop that seemed to have everything.

'Alan, go to Holmes' and get your grandad his tobacco.'

'Alan, go to Holmes' and get a mouse trap.'

'Alan, go to Holmes' and get a pair of shoe laces.'

Whenever my grandma wanted something, we got it from Holmes' shop – potatoes, bread, sliced meat, vegetables, sometimes biscuits and eggs. I was never given a ration card or money, just a list. The lady behind the counter would write something in a book, mark off the list and give it back to me. She always said the same thing, 'Give this list to your grandma, Alan.' I liked to go to Holmes' corner shop and to hear, 'It's little Alan; give him a pear drop,' or, 'Get Alan a mint ball out of the jar.' Sometimes, I was given a few broken biscuits.

It was the same when I was doing jobs for grandad. They were all outside jobs.

'Here, lad, come and watch this.'

I had to watch carefully, because he quite quickly told me to 'get on with it'.

'Right, lad, come here and I'll show you how to stake and tie my chrysanthemums.'

'Why do they need tying, Grandad?'

'Well, they need to be tied to the cane to keep them straight when it's windy.'

'But it's not windy in the greenhouse, so why have I got to stake and tie all them tomatoes?'

'Eee, lad, use your brains – it's obvious.'

'Um, so you don't have to bend down when they all droop onto the floor?'

'Don't use them clever words with me, lad. My tomatoes are so big and juicy they weigh the plant down, and if they lie on top of the soil, they rot, that's why they need staking. Right, then, let's get on with the chrysanthemums. I want you to make sure the cane is about a foot in the ground. And don't break any.'

'What if the ground's hard?'

'It won't be. I've dug it often enough, and there's a ton of horse muck in it.'

'Why have I to make sure that the canes are in a foot deep?'

'Because my chrysanthemums are that big and heavy they'll pull the canes over if they're not in deep enough.'

Sometimes, I would go too far.

'If I tie the string using a sheepshank or a reef knot, will you be able to undo it when you want to cut the flowers?'

'If you're not careful, I'll use my special string and tie up your tongue, and that'll hurt.'

'What do you mean, Grandad?'

'Just tie them flowers up in a knot and mind my canes.'

I knew when to just agree.

'All right, Grandad.'

He also taught me how to sweep the yard and path.

'It's that simple; you can get the brush and start.'

'Right, Grandad.'

'Oh, and don't forget to clean up the garden tools and put them in the shed.'

'Right, Grandad. Anything else?'

'Yes, but I'll tell you when you've done them jobs.'

I liked to see him sitting on his wicker seat, smoking his pipe while he watched me tidying up.

'Right, Grandad, both jobs are done. Can I go out and play now?'

'Not yet. I told you there would be another job, and anyone with any brains would see what it is.'

I could see my chance of playing out slowly fading. He was trying to be clever, but I hadn't to be cheeky.

'Grandad, can you just tell me the job?'

'All I can say is sweep the yard. You can't leave it like that. Look at all the soil on that path.'

I stared in the direction of his pointing finger, quickly realising that I'd brushed the yard and path, and only then cleaned the tools.

'Eee, Grandad, that was daft, wasn't it? I'll not do that again.'

'Right, lad.'

The most exciting job I did for my grandad was to go collecting horse manure. At the right hand corner of our field was the railway bridge. The horses, whether the coalman's or the milkman's, always stopped under the bridge for their feed or for a rest. So that is where I would fill the bucket. The bridge was close to our field, so I could fill it sometimes ten times over, which always pleased Grandad. That made me happy, but what I liked most about this job was to simply stand under the railway bridge. At that point, the train went very fast, often with an ear-piercing scream of its whistle. Down below, under the bridge, I closed my eyes in terror, hoping that the bridge wouldn't collapse. When I opened them, the scene was always the same: the horses either quietly munching from their feed bags or staring motionless straight ahead, and the milkman reading a newspaper or chatting to the coalman. As the noise faded out of existence, the scene under that railway bridge was always one of instant and welcome relief.

One job I was told to do was different. I had to go to one of my grandparents' relatives, who lived about a quarter of a mile from our house. We had run out of coal, so I knew why I was sent, but not why it had to be me who went to collect it. I was eight years old; it took some doing to carry a full bucket of coal that long distance. That's why I say I don't know why I was sent to do this job. Before I had gone five yards, I knew that I wouldn't make it. I carried that bucket first in the right hand, then the left, and then in both hands, and was soon crying. In my mind, I could see my grandparents waiting for me.

A few minutes later, I felt very proud of myself. I was still struggling along, right hand, left hand, both hands, but the bucket was now only about one quarter full. I had realised that if I hid some of the coal in the hedgerow and took the lighter weight home, then I could return for the next load. So this is how I carried the bucket of coal home. It took four trips. I told Grandma it was the only way I could manage to do it. She was just glad that I had brought the coal. I feel something was going on, that had forced Grandma to send me out for that bucket of coal, as if she wanted me out of the way.

Anyway, that job worried me, because I didn't want to do it again. The coal supply was built up during the summer months, but gradually dwindled during the winter. In the late summer or early autumn, when the coal shed was full, it was easy to take out a bucketful and hide it; this bucketful of coal I emptied and secretly hid in our field. If my grandma told me to go to the relatives for a bucketful of coal, I could now just bring it home from our field. Sadly, this was my last winter with my grandparents, and when I left, that bucketful of coal was still in our field.

# My Second Life

# The Man in the Dark Suit

Fried eggs and bacon, an unusual sight in Grandma's house, being hungrily devoured by a strange man dressed in a blue uniform. This man in blue is the earliest memory that I have of my dad. He had just returned from the war and he was my hero. I couldn't wait to hear about all his daredevil exploits. Why had he never come home? Had he been wounded? Had he been fighting in a far distant land? Had he ever been captured? To discover that he had spent the entire war in England was a big disappointment. This feeling quickly vanished when the story came out that whilst working on the barrage balloons, he had somehow been caught in the crossfire from German planes, and when he was racing for shelter in the bedlam and hail of bullets, one bullet shot off the heel of his boot. I had never realised that you could be so close to death. This revelation restored the admiration and hero-worship of my newfound father.

At the time, it didn't seem important that he had never come home to see me and Donald during those long and hard war years. Anyway, he disappeared again, but this time returned within a few weeks. This disappearing and returning happened a number of times. When he appeared, we were always ushered out of the room by our grandparents and told quite firmly to go out and play. Usually, he had once again disappeared when we returned to the house. On the rare occasion he was still there, he would find some pretext to ignore our presence. After these visits, my grandparents looked sad and were always very quiet. It didn't take long for my hero-worship to fade completely; this man, now in a dark suit, was still a stranger. I had begun to dislike the man in the dark suit, and now wanted the visits to stop.

Because this situation was upsetting me, my wheezing and bleeding days were not only happening more often, they were more severe. My grandparents took me to the infirmary for some allergy tests. This made me feel that something was seriously wrong. The first doctor asked numerous questions, and then I was taken by a severe looking nurse to another room, where she used my right arm as a scratch and scrape pad. Looking even more severe, and with a stern warning, the nurse said, ‘Please refrain from touching your right arm.’ I didn’t know what “refrain” meant, but I knew I hadn’t to touch my right arm.

A second doctor asked my grandparents more questions, after which, a contraption was placed on the table and the doctor demonstrated the correct procedures with regard to its use. It consisted of a dark brown glass phial with various protruding inlet and outlet connections and a light brown rubber tube with a balloon-type diaphragm at one end. At some place in the set-up of the apparatus was a space to hold a small quantity of liquid called Riddobron which could be released as a spray; this, when inhaled, would help to relieve my bronchial tubes, so reducing to some degree the severity of my asthma attacks. My grandparents, looking bewildered, silently nodded their understanding. We left that doctor’s room with my grandad holding the contraption as if it were a time bomb ready to explode.

It was now back to the first doctor. My right forearm had become unrecognisable; the scratches and scrapes had had their effect. The results showed a violent reaction to fish, followed closely by nuts, dust and animal hair. The doctor didn’t mince his words: ‘If you ever want to kill yourself, just go and live on a desert island where all there is to eat are coconuts and fish.’ Grandma may have struggled with contraptions, but this was plainly familiar territory. She needed no further persuasion; the daily dose of cod liver oil instantly stopped, which for me, meant the visit to the hospital had been a success.

The visit must have ranked as important, because it was rare for my grandparents to leave the familiar and comfortable surroundings of our field. It is the final memory I have of their love, kindness and sense of responsibility for me. The normal everyday comforts still continued, but this episode highlights their concern. The introduction of Riddobron and the exclusion of cod liver oil helped, so their efforts were not in vain. Donald wasn’t pleased, as he still had to have his cod liver oil; I made things worse by suggesting he could have mine as well.

The root causes of the worsening asthma and eczema were anxiety and nervous tension, brought about by the man in the dark suit. This was something my grandparents were not able to prevent. He was still appearing and disappearing.

Now my "next life" was near. I had been told that my dad was going to remarry, and I was to leave my grandparents and go to live with them. My grandparents had done their best to prepare me for this, but on the day I left them, I lost control; I tried to hide, then I started to scream and fight. I must have increased their suffering with these reactions, and the sight of me being lifted and carried bodily away from them, down that unevenly-flagged garden path, would have remained an awful memory for them.

# Changes

My next life began; I was eight years old, unprepared, exhausted and in shock.

I wasn't thrashed, though sometimes smacked and often pushed about, as well as being frequently shouted at. My parents didn't show me any love, tenderness or kindness. I was rarely called by my name. Their tone of voice indicated that it was me who was being addressed; their manner would be one of snappy impatience, threats or, at the very best, curt requests that had to be carried out without complaint.

I blamed it all on this stranger with the prominent front teeth, my dad's new wife. She didn't look like a wicked witch; she was small and slim, with dark brown hair and brown eyes, and without those teeth, she probably could have been classed as pretty.

I always seemed to be in her way, and was made to feel insignificant. For example, at the first mealtime, I noticed that only two chairs were available.

'Don't sit on the chairs,' came her sharp voice.

'What do you mean?'

'I mean them chairs are for me and your dad.'

'Where do I sit, then?'

'That's your place' – pointing to a corner of the table – 'and you can stand up, it won't do you any harm.'

'But I'll be stretching up to eat my food. I can't eat standing up. I can't – '

'Quiet! That's your place.'

'Can I sit on the armchair?'

'No! That's Donald's place.'

'But what about the chairs in the front – '

'Listen, will you! For the umpteenth time, that's your place, and I don't want any of your lip, right?'

So, for the next twelve months, when we all sat down at the table, I was the one always standing up.

It was the same when they settled down in the evening, in front of the fire. If I stayed in the room and plucked up enough courage to sit on the floor near the warmth of the fire, the response would be immediate.

'Get over there, out of the way,' one of them would snap, with an impatient gesture directing me to the farthest corner of the room.

'But it's cold over there.'

'Listen, just get over there. I want some peace and quiet when I've been at it all day.'

Children should be seen and not heard – or, in my case, children should not be heard, and preferably not even seen. This and "out of sight, out of mind" were their main rules for bringing me up. It didn't take me long to realise that this worked two ways, and consequently, whatever the weather, I only had to say, 'I'm going out to play.' Since there was usually no response, I could just disappear. I wasn't lonely, but felt much happier and strangely more secure when away from the house and playing with my friends, the same friends I had known in my first life.

These friends were still nearby because, after the war, my dad returned to live in the house he owned, where I had spent the first three years of my life; this house was only five minutes' walk away from my grandparents'.

My dad made things plain on the first day.

'Come here, Alan, I want a word with you. Right, listen to me, this is where you're living now, and I don't want you to go spending all your time at your grandad's house.'

'Why not?'

'Because they want a rest. They've been moaning about how hard it's been with you and Donald, and they've told me they've had enough. Anyway, you can't keep being carried down that garden path, screaming and bawling.'

I stared in disbelief. 'I don't believe you! My grandma was crying every time you came in that black suit. She didn't want you to come.'

'Listen, that's enough. I'm only going to tell you this once. You can play out, but you don't go playing on that field near your grandad's. If I see you on that field, you won't be playing out at all.'

'But I want to see my grandma. If you let me see her, I won't scream and bawl.'

'I've told you, they've had enough. Why can't you be like Donald? He just said OK.'

'He shouldn't say OK, it's not proper English.' This was what Grandma used to say.

'Listen, Alan, your new mother wants to see you settling down. This is your new home.'

'She's not my mother. Let me – '

'Right, I've had enough. Just go up to your bedroom. And remember, I'm warning you, don't go playing on that field, or else.'

But I did go on that field. The next few months would see me furtively crossing it and sneaking up that familiar garden path, feeling a surge of relief once inside the house.

I went, that first time, hoping my dad's words weren't true.

'Hello, Grandma, I've come to visit you.'

'Oh, Alan, what a nice surprise. Let me tell your grandad. Just sit down. Eee, I'm glad to see you.'

When Grandad came in, he seemed tired; it looked as if my dad had been telling the truth.

'Eee, Polly, put the kettle on. Let's all have a nice cup of tea.'

'Grandad, my dad said you'd had enough of me and Donald and you wanted a rest. He said, I haven't to play on our field and I'm not to see you, but I want to. I had to sneak up our garden path. I was worried that my dad was telling the truth about you not wanting to see me.'

'Here, Alan, here's a nice spoonful of malt.'

'Eee, thanks, Grandma. I'm glad I've come.'

'Listen, Alan, you can come and visit us any time you want, but you'll have to be careful your dad doesn't find out, or else he'll be angry. If I'm not in, I'll only be at Mrs Whitaker's, but your grandad will be in. He'll be hiding in his greenhouse as usual.'

‘And don’t tell anyone.’ Grandad sounded serious. ‘Once you’ve told somebody, it’s not a secret anymore. Just keep quiet, lad.’

‘Right, Grandad, I will. Grandma, if you’re out, is it all right if Grandad gives me a spoonful of malt?’ I liked it when he gave me the malt, as he always gave me a bigger spoonful.

‘Yes, of course, Alan. Eee, I’m really glad you sneaked up our garden path.’

So the secret visits continued, and I became very clever at working my way through the field and into Grandad’s front garden.

One day, though, came a shock. I walked into the living room and saw Donald. We stared at each other; he managed to speak first.

‘Eee, Alan, what have you come here for? My dad will kill you if he finds out.’

‘He won’t find out unless you tell him.’ I was still trying to grasp what had happened.

‘I won’t tell him. He doesn’t know I’m here, either.’

It turned out that Donald had also been sneaking across the field to our grandparents; they hadn’t told either of us about the other one because, as Grandad said, ‘You’ve just got to keep quiet, lad.’

Donald wasn’t very happy about my visits; he thought I was too young to keep a secret. It was only when he realised I’d been able to keep all my previous visits from him that he was convinced.

This is how my second life began.

# Saturday Night Out

In these early months, my parents always went out on Saturday nights. I had to go to bed before the baby-sitter arrived. On one such Saturday night, I was sent to bed, sore with eczema and breathing with difficulty, as was now usual. Despite curling myself up into the tightest possible ball and wrapping myself in the blanket, I still lay shivering in the cold bed. Never having seen the baby-sitter, and unable to escape from the shivering and a feeling of desperation, I decided to turn to this stranger for help. I crept quietly down the stairs, trembling with fright. As I began to open the door, muffled sounds came from inside the room, filling me with alarm. I tried to stop the door, but it swung open on its squeaking hinges. The room was lit only by the fire glow, which seemed to dance towards the outer edges, casting shadowy, flickering looming shapes into every corner. The area in front of the fire shone bright and clear, revealing a man and woman lying naked on the floor. I thought that the fire must have been so warm and inviting that they had to take off their clothes. Suddenly, I heard the man's voice shouting.

I stammered the words, 'Can I have a hot brick to warm me up?'

He stood up and moved towards me in a menacing fashion. He looked like an animal. I had never seen a naked man before, and this man, towering over me in the shadowy light, seemed like a great, hairy giant. I turned and ran up the stairs to hide under the bed. I stayed there, numb with fright, for what seemed like an age. Eventually, I heard my parents enter the house; soon after the strangers left. A short time later, my parents went to bed, and I crawled back under the freezing blanket. I never saw those people again. In fact, we never had a baby-sitter again.

Not having a baby-sitter didn't prevent my parents from going out. My father had a large black motor car with running boards. This car, which usually had to be crank-started, always looked and sounded old and weary; when it finally broke down permanently, it was left in the street. For a few weeks that winter, while it was still running, Donald and I spent Saturday nights inside it. We were placed in the back seats and, having been driven to a street near to the social event, the car was parked and left, with us two boys in the dark, under strict orders to stay in the back and keep quiet. In the wintry weather, we soon became cold and miserable.

We each had a pocket watch, given to us by our grandad from the public house, so on Saturday nights, we slipped them into our pockets and then slipped ourselves out of the car, knowing we could gauge the time to return to the car before our parents came back. I felt very confident and comfortable with my brother, though on the Saturday nights, walking around those busy Wigan town centre streets, I hardly let go of his hand.

The pavements were crowded with people jostling for position, all heading in different directions. Many of them, attracted by the welcoming warmth of the brightly lit shop windows displaying their tempting goods, would stop abruptly to stand and stare and hope and plan and dream. Others would stop, waiting impatiently for an opportunity to cross the busy road, a dangerous venture on a wide expanse of smoke-filled streams of slow-moving buses and cars.

'Donald, I'm frightened. Let's go back to the car.'

'We're OK, Alan. Just hold my hand all the time; don't let go for a second.' Donald's voice was calm and reassuring; I felt safe now, and soon was able to enjoy the sights and sounds.

'Eee, Donald, isn't this super fun! It's better than in daylight,' I said excitedly.

'Just be careful of the drunks.'

'How can you tell when people are drunk?'

'Look at their faces and watch them walking. Their faces don't look normal, and they can't walk in a straight line, or they bump into people and laugh.'

I held Donald's hand even more tightly.

I was about eight years old at the time and Donald was nearly twelve. This is the last real shared memory I have of my brother and me. I never again held his hand. Shortly after this experience, a gulf opened up between us. I stayed a little boy and Donald became a youth. Perhaps experiencing the sights of the town centre on a Saturday night had more of an awakening effect on Donald, speeding up his sudden change. So, until the car broke down permanently, Saturday nights, thanks to Donald, had become very enjoyable. We were always sitting quietly, sometimes pretending to be asleep, when our parents came back to the car.

The inevitable demise of the car did not stop the Saturday night social activity. The warmer days and lighter nights had arrived, so we were left on our own in the house with strict orders to stay in and not answer the door to anyone. In fact, I was always sent off to bed before my parents left. Donald was allowed to stay up for a little while, but never to leave the house. This seemed satisfactory, and it was very unusual for anything out of the ordinary to happen. But something did.

A reaction to the change from one life to another set in, and every Saturday night, it was released. I would be lying in bed with the windows open and the birds singing when I started to cry. The crying changed to screaming and then hysterical shouting. Donald pleaded with me to stop, but I wasn't able to. The previous summer, I knew nothing about this life. I was happy. I was safe. Now I was shouting and screaming for this early life to return. These Saturday nights went on for quite a while, but somehow, I eventually managed to control my reaction, though there was not one Saturday night that, having quietly and obediently gone off to bed, I didn't silently cry myself to sleep.

# A Dreadful Day

I noticed that my stepmother was getting bigger. Even though my aim was to keep her out of sight as much as possible, I couldn't help wondering what was wrong with her. While hiding in dark corners or behind half-closed doors, I heard things: 'When do you think it will be…? It'll happen when you least expect it…I hope it's on time.' These words seemed to establish in my little mind that she would finally burst.

Suddenly, when she had reached a gigantic size, without exploding, I was sent away to stay with relatives. Relatives I never knew existed. The auntie was my dad's sister; she was kind and gentle. The uncle was gruff and frightening; I kept out of his way. This stay was much more pleasant and enjoyable than life with my parents. However, after about only two weeks, I was returned to my parents, disconsolate but also excited. As I approached the house, this feeling of anticipation increased. Had the balloon burst? I ran into the house and was immediately faced with my stepmother, who looked to have returned to normal size. She was holding an object wrapped, completely hidden, in a white shawl. Whatever was in there, she was speaking to it. Her mannerisms and tone of voice were kind and soothing, completely alien to her approach towards me.

'You have a brother. Do not go near him!'

These abrupt words were my introduction to my half-brother.

A few weeks after he was born, we moved to Hindley, five miles and two bus journeys away from my grandparents; this information came from the removal man when I was sitting in his van. It was all happening so quickly that I hadn't realised we were moving; I should have known when the motor car vanished and some large, empty wooden boxes appeared. When we arrived amidst the chaos, I was told to keep Keith quiet by pushing him in his pram in the backyard. It was a big pram, and it was hard to steer it straight.

It still hadn't properly sunk in that we'd moved, and I was struggling to understand what was happening. In this sort of situation, I would normally ask for Donald's help, but he hadn't been around for a while. He must have been with my dad, I thought. Unusual things, though, had been happening lately. When I had gone to my auntie's for those two weeks, it was without Donald, and when I came back, he wouldn't tell me where he'd been. He was now at the secondary modern school, and definitely growing up. Then he'd disappeared several times overnight, sometimes two nights.

'Where do you keep going?'

'I'm not telling you.'

'Please, Donald, I want to know where you keep going.'

'I'm not telling you. I'm not telling anybody. So you don't need to ask Gerrard or Eric or any of my other friends. Like my grandad's told us, don't tell anybody, just keep quiet.'

It was more than idle curiosity. If Donald was able to escape then why not me? So I persisted.

'But Donald, I don't like it here, especially when I'm on my own. Let me come with you.'

He relented, up to a point. 'Listen, Alan, it's all to do with the big school. I can't tell you anything else. Please don't keep asking me.'

I don't know whether he was becoming upset, or just fed up with me, but that's when I stopped quizzing him.

So, here I now was in a different town, pushing Keith's pram, and Donald once again was nowhere to be seen. When my stepmother appeared at the back door, checking on my pram skills, I took my opportunity.

'Where's Donald?'

'He isn't living with us anymore.'

'What do you mean?' I stared in disbelief.

'He's gone living at a relative's house near his school. He'll be there till he leaves.'

'But that'll be years. That's ages. I want to see my brother. You can't do this.'

'Listen, don't ever tell me what I can't do, you cheeky imp. Just wait till your dad comes in.'

With that, she disappeared back into the house.

Of course, when he finally arrived, Donald wasn't with him. I had been clinging to the hope of seeing him again, thinking and hoping that my stepmother was just being wicked. But these hopes were dashed, and if a little boy has such a thing as spirit then at that point it was crushed.

My stepmother spoke immediately.

'He's been nagging me all day about Donald. I told you to tell him. Why do you always leave it to me? Well, go on then, tell him. And tell him not to be so cheeky.'

'What have you been up to?' My dad was stern and unforgiving.

'Nothing. I just asked where Donald was and she went mad.'

'Don't call your mother "she".' He was getting angry.

'She's not my mother.'

'Get up to your room! Quick!'

'I don't know where it is. I've been pushing that stupid pram for ages.'

'Just get upstairs, out of the road.'

That was always my dad's way of facing up to friction in the house.

All I wanted was to go back to my grandparents, if only for a visit. They were five miles away, a short bus journey to the familiar and friendly surroundings of Wigan town centre, an easy journey. I went back downstairs to face him.

'I thought I told you to get upstairs.'

'Can I go and see my grandma and grandad?'

'No, it's too far away and too awkward.'

'I can catch a bus straight to Wigan, and I know Wigan like the back of my hand,' I said, trying to be clever.

'Listen, lad, I don't want you to ask me again. This is your new life. Why don't you settle down?'

'I don't want to live here. Anyway, I don't like her, and I never will.'

'Right, that's enough.'

'I want to see my grandma. Why don't you let me see my grandma?' I was losing control.

‘Right, just get back up them stairs quick, and stay up there this time.’

And so it was that for the next two and a half years I didn’t see Donald. In that one dreadful day, I had lost the comforting influences of my brother and my grandparents. My parents didn’t seem to care.

That first night, without Donald to help me, I lay in my new room, closed my eyes and went back to see my grandparents. I walked up the lobby into an empty room. I knew what to do. Straight to the greenhouse. I could see Grandad replacing some tomato canes. He didn’t see me.

‘Hello, Grandad,’ I said sadly.

‘Eee, Alan, don’t creep up on me like that. I’m getting too old.’

‘I’m sorry, Grandad, but I’m fed up.’

‘What’s wrong, lad?

‘We’ve moved house. It’s five miles away. They’ve sent Donald somewhere else and now I’m on my own and they keep shouting at me. I don’t like them, Grandad. Can I come back here?’

‘Listen, Alan, your grandma will be in soon. She can make us something to eat and you can tell us all about it, all right?’

‘OK, Grandad. Can I help you to do your jobs while we’re waiting?’

‘OK, lad. You know what to do. I’ll just sit in the wicker chair and smoke my pipe.’ I think he liked to say OK when my grandma wasn’t around.

‘I bet you’ve forgotten what to do.’

‘I haven’t, Grandad. Your jobs are so easy, I can do them with my eyes shut.’

‘Eee, Alan, thar a rum lad.’

It felt good to hear my grandad puffing and chuckling.

Grandma finally arrived back from Mrs Whitaker’s.

‘Eee, it’s Alan. What a nice surprise.’

‘I’ve come because I’m fed up, Grandma.’

‘Come and help me to make your grandad’s tea and tell me what’s been happening.’

‘We’ve moved house. It’s five miles away. They’ve sent Donald somewhere else and now I’m on my own and they keep shouting at me. I don't like them, Grandma. Please can I come back here?'

'You can come and see us any time you want, Alan. Now, after our tea, I'll give you a big spoonful of malt and you can sit close to me and we'll watch Grandad nodding off next to our lovely warm fire.'

I looked at her, and then was suddenly speaking – 'Grandma, there's nothing like a spoonful of malt to make you feel better.'

# A Welcome Reprieve

I had made up my mind not to like my stepmother before I even saw her. When my second life started, there was no doubt that she too must have had a difficult task, having to put up with a stubborn, sullen child who would not accept her as a mother. But I can't think of one instant, one gesture, of love or even kindness from her which might have changed my attitude.

When my half-brother Keith came onto the scene, I saw a different side to her nature. She was tender, gentle, caring and comforting with him, whereas I was treated like an alien being, completely excluded from all her affections. It was plain that she loved Keith, so what were her true feelings towards me? Whatever they were, I knew that my presence in those early years irritated her. I was better out of sight, so out of sight I went.

I soon met other children in the neighbourhood; being small and thin, I never threatened their positions, and was usually welcome to join in their games. They played nothing, though, but football. The difficulty for me was the footwear; they all wore clogs, and I had only thin, flimsy, down-at-heel shoes. In the early days, I was often kicked and bruised by those hard clogs, but gradually became more nimble and efficient at dodging them, while at the same time still able to control the ball. So much so that it became well known in the area that here was a blossoming football prospect – 'If only he could put on a bit of weight and grow a bit taller.' Apart from football, which I often practised on my own, I didn't do anything. The next two years drifted by, with me doing my best to stay out of sight as much as possible.

The continual rejection was having an effect; I lost interest in school work, but because it was easy and because I remained quiet, and obedient, I came out top of the class, eventually passing the eleven plus, a real achievement, leading to a coveted place at grammar school. The day the letter arrived, my stepmother opened it, read the contents, turned to me and simply said, 'You passed that test.' When my dad came home from work, she gave him the letter without speaking. I was sitting on one of the two available chairs at the table, having my tea. He read the letter, then spoke.

'Go to the shop and get me twenty Players.'

This I did, leaving my half-finished meal to go cold. When I came back, he had left the room, and I didn't see him again that night. A few days later, I plucked up courage to speak to him.

'Mrs Dowling was very pleased with me for passing the eleven plus.'

'I bet she didn't offer to pay for it all,' my stepmother said.

'What do you mean?'

'I mean it's money for uniforms, money for shirts, money for pants, money for shoes, and even money for a daft school bag. I wish you hadn't passed that stupid test.'

'Well, I did. I could have passed it with my eyes shut. Anyway, I was talking to my dad.'

'You cheeky imp!' she shouted. 'Get out of the room!' She turned to my dad. 'See, I've to put up with this all day.'

I looked at my dad. 'I only want to tell you what Mrs Dowling said. She said I'd done well. Only three of us passed. She said she hoped my parents were proud of me.'

'What did you say?' These were the first words my dad had spoken to me since he'd sent me for cigarettes, several days previously.

'I just said thank you. I didn't know what else to say.'

'Why not?'

'Because I don't know where I am in this house. You read the letter and then disappeared, and I'm left eating my cold tea. Just tell me, have I done well, passing the eleven plus?'

'Listen, lad, it's not just about passing a test. Why don't you—'

'Have I done well? Are you proud of me?'

'Don't interrupt me. You're supposed to be intelligent, so start showing it. I was going to give you some advice. Why don't you settle down and be more pleasant to your mother?'

'She's not my mother.'

‘Shut up and listen to me. These are difficult times and she’s trying her best. It’ll be very expensive to send you to the grammar school, but you passed so I’ll make sure you go.’

‘But I’m not bothered about going.’

‘Right, lad, get that out of your head straight away. You passed that test so you’re going.’

After all this, my first journey to grammar school was a nervous one. I would certainly be the smallest boy in the school. I wondered if this would make a difference. The idea of facing scornful bullies filled me with dismay, but despite being lightweight and obviously weak spirited, I felt capable, even then, of generally holding my own.

My parents had begrudgingly purchased the grammar school’s basic requirements. I looked smart and clean, wearing a cap, black blazer with school badge, short grey pants, white shirt and black and white striped tie, with a satchel stretching across from my left shoulder; all this gave me a strange but comforting feeling. I also felt some reassurance on that first journey with the thought that school work would not be too difficult.

Any fears soon disappeared. The grammar school gave me renewed energy, although I quickly discovered that the classroom subjects were not so easy. Surprisingly, this seemed to lift my spirits; now I needed to concentrate in class or else lag behind. I would no longer be top of the class. At the end of the first term, my placement, only tenth in the class, gave me a wonderful sense of achievement.

The outside activities and PT in the school gymnasium, I loved. The gym lessons would now be classified as old-fashioned or even dangerous, but they were exciting, and I excelled in them. Climbing ropes, balancing six feet above the floor or walking along the wooden beam, climbing wall-bars and jumping off springboards to vault over the leather-bound wooden horse took me back to my early life with my grandparents. Even my “hard-to-breathe” days could not stop me from participating.

The playing fields seemed huge, but I wasn’t overwhelmed. My football skills caught the teacher’s eye in my first term. He seemed to think I might be good enough for the junior team, normally made up from third years, by the start of my second year.

The first overwhelming feeling of joy came during a practice match, when, after wriggling around two burly defenders in the muddy penalty area, in order to keep my balance, I had held the shirt of one of them, enabling me to move forward and score. The referee, our sports teacher, blew his whistle to disallow the goal; it was his reason why that gave me this joy – 'Right, class, here we have an excellent footballer (meaning me!), but we must realise we are not allowed to score goals using our hands.' All the time, he was looking at me, but smiling.

The pattern was set. I was beginning to settle down. Eager to tell my grandparents, I went to see them in the only way I could. I found a quiet place and closed my eyes.

'Where's Grandma?'

'She's gone to Mrs Whitaker's with a custard pie. She'll be back in a minute.'

'Right, Grandad. I'll tell you while she's not here. Everything's OK; I like going to school, but I'm not top of the class.'

'I'm glad you like it, Alan, but I'll tell you something, there must be a lot of clever lads in your class if you're not top.'

'There are some really clever lads, Grandad, but the cleverest ones are the girls. There were seven girls in the top ten.'

'What position were you, lad?'

'Tenth.'

'Eee, lad, you've not done so bad. Oh, here's your grandma.'

'Hello, Alan. Have you come for your tea?'

'I just thought I'd let you know I'm settling down. I was tenth in the class.'

'There was seven girls in the top ten,' Grandad said.

'It must be a clever school if you're not top of the class.'

'Thanks, Grandma. It's really great. Oh, and I've been told I'll soon be in the school football team. The games teacher said I'll be playing inside right, and that's my favourite position.'

'That's good, lad. Right, Polly, let's all have our tea. I'm glad you've come and told us how you're getting on. We were worried about you, weren't we, Grandma?'

'Yes, but I knew he'd be all right.'

So I stayed for my tea, read an old comic, had a spoonful of malt and left with Grandad's words in my ears – 'Beat them girls, lad!'

In all aspects of school life, academic and sporting, I was comfortable. They seemed to alleviate all the strain and tension at home. The gulf between school life and home life widened to such an extent that even, as the Christmas holiday began, I was longing to be back at school again. Imagine a boy of eleven not looking forward to school holidays!

The spring term continued in the same fashion.

The start of the summer term saw the beginning of the cricket season, which for first year boys mainly consisted, thankfully, of practising in the nets. I say thankfully because it was very unlikely that my parents would have gone so far as to purchase cricket flannels, sweater and boots for the occasional organised school match. It was during this summer term in the cricket nets that it was first suggested I should concentrate on bowling slow leg breaks and googlies. Obviously fast or medium paced bowling was out of the question, and I seemed to find great difficulty as a batsman. My defensive technique was reasonably sound, but my attacking strokes were virtually non-existent; even though my timing was satisfactory, I was never able to put any power or venom into the shots.

My favourite activity was to practise slip field catching, using the "cradle". The slatted boat-shaped wooden structure was designed so that a cricket ball thrown into it diverted in unpredictable directions, at speed, giving you the opportunity to jump and dive to catch the ball at full stretch with either hand. This was marvellous fun, and being nimble and agile, I finally got the hang of catching the ball and became a more than useful slip fielder. I had played cricket during the summertime when I lived with my grandparents, but nothing like this. This was organised cricket with every opportunity to improve.

The summer term brought another pleasant surprise, in that the school sent us to the local swimming baths. I had never been to a swimming baths before, but fortunately, though I had never been in the water since the escapade in the sea at Blackpool when I nearly drowned, I was not afraid. I did struggle to keep afloat, but was not the only one floundering in the water. After several sessions, instead of going straight down, I managed to more or less splash my way across one breadth of the baths. It's funny sometimes that you never forget what turns out to be the last words in a normal routine which, at the time, you assume will be continuing as usual next day or next week. The swimming instructor's last words to me were, 'It won't be long now before you cut down the splashes, and start swimming a length. You'll soon be swimming like Johnny Weissmuller.' I'm afraid his prediction was wrong.

## The Clown of the Class

In my home life I was never told about things until they were just about to happen or had actually happened. It had been obvious that we were going to move to another house because of all the packing cases in the rooms, but I hadn't imagined how much my life was about to be turned upside down.

It happened one Friday evening, when, coming home from school feeling good, I was flattened by terrible news.

'Tomorrow we'll be moving. You'll be travelling in the removal van. Next week, you'll be starting another school.'

With a sudden feeling of helplessness, I went upstairs. That night, I was left to my own devices. I stayed in my room and cried myself to sleep.

The following day, I found myself in the removal van with the driver and his mate. The van seemed to be straining and grumbling, exerting all its influence towards breaking my heart, a heart which was already broken; I would never again be going to the school which, in a few short months, had given me back my strength.

We arrived. The furniture van left.

'Where are we living?'

'Here.'

'Where are we?'

'We're in Leyland.'

'How far is it from Hindley?'

'It's a long way.'

'Why could we not have stayed in Hindley?'

'Ask your dad, it's him that wanted to come here. Don't keep asking questions, just get on with unpacking them cases.'

My dad finally appeared, and I spoke to him at once.

'Why have we come living here?'

'Because I've got a job here. So has your brother.'

'What do you mean?'

'I mean, this is where we're living because this is where me and Donald are working.'

'Is Donald coming back?'

'Yes, next month.'

The news of Donald's return didn't seem important at that moment.

'Why can't I go to my school? I don't want to move here.'

'Listen, lad, you're starting a different school on Monday and I'm starting work without having to travel miles every day.'

'I'm not going.'

'Don't start, or else you know what you'll get.'

'I want to go back to Hindley. You won't let me see my grandma, and now we've moved here and I can't go to my school. I'll never like it here and I don't like you!'

'Just get up to your room quick. I'm writing a letter, and when you get to school on Monday, make sure you hand it in to a teacher.'

'I'm not going and if I do, I'll rip up that stupid letter.'

I had never before shown such defiance as I did that first Saturday afternoon in Leyland, but it didn't alter anything.

'Right, this is bloody ridiculous. I've only just got in. You'd better get out of my sight quick or you'll get belted!' I gazed, hypnotised, at his big fist.

He had become very angry; my defiance weakened fast. I went upstairs.

I started a new grammar school. There were about four weeks left of the summer term; in that time, I felt very inept and completely out of place. My grandma would describe my sad state as being 'like a fish out of water'. In these four long and difficult weeks, I was made to feel more uncomfortable.

'We're nearly in the second year. Why have you come here with two years left at junior school?'

'You're just a stupid little kid.'

'My brother's bigger than you, and he's only seven.'

'Where have you come from, Lilliput?'

It was mainly taunts and jibes, though some boys were more threatening.

'Pump up my bike tyres or I'll inform the prefects and you'll be severely punished.'

'Tidy up the inside of my desk. Do it properly or we'll throw your books all over the room every morning.'

'Go and get my coat from peg 23 as soon as the bell goes. Bring it straight back to the classroom.'

In that first month, I never resisted these bullies or complained to a teacher. I remained silent and obediently did as I was told. The bullying ended at the start of the second year. It probably had been just a peer test to gauge my reaction. If that was the case, this test was the only one I passed in my four-year stay at the school.

The reappearance of Donald came at the end of that horrible month. Alas, this caused me to feel even more insecure. I couldn't believe my eyes when I first saw him. He looked like a stranger, like a young man. He was never tall, but at that moment, he towered over me. He was much heavier-boned than me and looked sturdy and strong. His brown eyes and dark brown hair enhanced his general appearance. On top of all that, he proudly announced to me that he had started shaving. He had grown up.

Donald was only fifteen or sixteen, but he was setting out his stall for the future. He was starting work as an apprentice turner at Leyland Motors, spending his time entirely in the tool room section, where the really skilled apprentices were placed. He progressed through the Ordinary National Certificate to obtain the Higher National Certificate, and his abilities were recognised later when he was transferred to staff, and worked on the organisation side of the tool room as a planner and industrial engineer.

We now had nothing in common.

'Hello, Donald. You look different.' I was struggling for something to say.

'Yes, Alan, it's great leaving school and starting work. How are you doing?'

'Oh, I'm OK.'

'How's school these days?'

'Oh, it's OK.'

'Are you in the football team?'

'No, they play rugby. Listen, Donald, have you got any jobs to do? We could help each other and do things together.'

'All I've got to do is to help to wash up the pots after meals. Anyway, I'll be going out most nights to night school, or out with my mates.'

'You seem to have everything planned.'

'I have, Alan. Listen, there's nothing I can do to change your situation. I'm just keeping quiet.'

Not many words were spoken, but I realised in that moment that I couldn't turn to my brother for help or comfort.

In those early weeks of the second year, I remained despondent and uninterested in schoolwork. My behaviour in class became increasingly silly to the point of being absurd. When I wasn't simply dreaming the lessons away, I could always find a willing partner to play noughts and crosses or other games, including a cricket game ("Owzat!") which involved rolling small metal hexagons indicating runs scored and different ways to be out. I sent notes to girls, flicked ink at boys trying to work and wrote lines given to me by prefects for out-of-class offences such as not wearing my school cap or running in the corridor.

The end of term and yearly reports would include such apt summaries of my work as:

'He thinks he is the clown of the class. Believe me, he *is* the clown of the class.'

'Liable to pest control, if one can be found that is strong enough.'

My timetable was split in two. During the entire four years, in most of the subjects, the lesson time was spent in acting the fool and covering the whole gamut of scorn and contempt, with a complete disregard for subject and teacher. A few subjects were approached with restrained enthusiasm and modest success. Essentially, it had now come down to three factors:

Was I frightened of the teacher? Did I actually like the teacher? Did I like the subject? If one or more of these applied, I would put in the modest effort which resulted in the modest success.

The sporting timetable for winter games was a disaster. My football prowess became nullified when, to my dismay, I discovered that it was a rugby union school. In the winter, apart from cross-country runs, the outside activity was rugby. Since I was unable to show off my football skills, and knowing that I could never succeed at rugby, the winter games lessons were awful. Despite my frailties, I managed to play some part in the class rugby games; being very quick with my feet – this had somehow been noticed – I was always selected as hooker for the class team. At that time, and at this extremely amateurish level, the ball was religiously thrown straight between the lines of prop forwards and hookers. It was my job to hook the ball back into my team's possession. My success rate over the four years was well over 75%. However, that was the sum total of my input. I normally languished somewhere on the field near to the action, watching and waiting until the whistle was blown for another scrum. I can't remember making one tackle or scoring one try in all those years. In fact, it was only by mistake that I ever handled the ball, and when I did, it was soon discarded. My limitations were revealed in the scrum down. I had to put my left arm around the shoulder of one burly prop forward and my right arm around the shoulder of another. If they both stood up to their full height, I dangled at least a foot from the ground. Playing rugby was a complete misplacement of talent, and my football skills faded.

The cricket seasons came and went. I was regularly praised for my ability to spin the leg-break viciously and to hide the googly successfully, but the school team always remained a closed shop. Each year the games master mustered up some encouraging words, usually ending with the same two pearls of wisdom, 'Keep practising,' and, 'England needs a good leg-break and googly bowler.'

These light-hearted comments gave me the inspiration to practise harder. He was one of the teachers who fitted into my three-factor analysis; in fact, he fitted all three. First, I was frightened of him, having watched him, in my early days at the school, thrash one of the pupils. His face had turned purple with rage, the boy suffering terribly for his misdemeanours. Secondly, I loved the indoor activities offered in the school gymnasium; these were similar to those I had experienced at my first grammar school, so they were familiar, and I knew that I could put on a good show. Being chosen to go to Liverpool to watch the Danish gymnastic team perform was the highlight of my school life. Thirdly, my gymnastic skills and cricket potential created a favourable impression on the games master, so I was treated well in comparison to other boys, many of whom received harsh treatment, verbal and physical. When he was in one of his rages,

I went back to being frightened of him, but, knowing that I was a boy instilled in the better side of his nature, I ended up liking the games master.

# Spot the Difference

I was in the enviable position, according to some boys who had to accomplish menial tasks before being allowed out to play, of being told regularly to, 'Get out of sight.' It wasn't unusual for me to get home from school, have my skimpy meal eaten quickly as instructed, complete any homework, go out to play, and by eight o'clock be in bed, without speaking a single word to either of my parents.

'He's sulking again,' one of them would say, but what else could I do in the face of their indifference?

This was during the days at my first grammar school; their complete lack of interest in me meant that I was left to do whatever I wanted; since I enjoyed school, this included working hard at my studies. I had no jobs to do in the house, and was free to concentrate on homework, which was always done and handed in on time, and to revise for any tests. I looked forward to after-school activities, which for me were football practice and the occasional "real" game on a Saturday morning. Since my parents were oblivious to my interests, the gap between home life and life at my first grammar school, widened.

The second grammar school was different. My home life changed at an alarming rate. The most dedicated skivvy would not have remained in their service. The list of household chores forced upon me was endless. They were all, at first, 'after school', but it didn't take long until 'before school' chores were added to the list. My stepmother, having some form of evening employment, reminded me daily that she was now going out to work 'through necessity' and that I must 'knuckle down'. 'Knuckling down' consisted of preparing all the vegetables for tea, setting the table, clearing the table and washing up. At some point every week, I cleaned the brasses and the front room window, mangled the washing and hung the clothes on the line or on the maiden. Usually, every day, there were errands to the local shops; Saturday morning was always two or three shops with two or three lists, followed by a visit to the gasworks, pulling a makeshift four-wheeled trolley. This, heavily laden with a very large bag of coke, was pulled, heaved and coaxed back to the house; there the coke was mixed with the more expensive coal to save money.

One of my early morning chores was to clean out the grate and light a fresh fire, having made sure on the previous evening that I had filled the coal bucket and chopped the firewood. This was obtained from discarded orange boxes that I had collected and carried home from the local shop.

Generally, the evening jobs had to be completed before six o'clock, because that was when my stepmother went to work. From the moment she left the house until her return two hours later, I had to look after Keith. At first, I thought I hated him, but in fact, over the years, I got to quite like him. He was a small, dark-haired lad who never seemed to do anything exciting. I regularly threatened to thump him, especially after a disagreement with my stepmother, but never did. My one regret, though, is the number of times I clipped the back of his head. It usually happened when his mother had made me angry or fed up, my reaction being to take it out on poor Keith. I used to call him thick and stupid, and play a game with him where I counted up to ten in French and then he had to do the same. The moment he got a number wrong, I would clip him on the back of his head, sometimes quite hard, the number of blows corresponding to the wrong number. This was a wicked thing to do, and Keith must have suffered terribly.

He didn't want to play at football or cricket. In the summer evenings, I quickly sorted him out.

'Right, Keith, bring everything you need.'

'OK, Alan. Will you make a space for parking?'

'Anything else?'

'No.'

'Well, hurry up, I want to play cricket.'

'Right, Alan.'

While he collected all his paraphernalia, I went around to "the backs" of the house to prepare the ground. "The backs" was five yards width of compacted cinder and ash mix, stretching the entire length between two streets. By the time Keith had arrived, I would have more or less completed my task.

'Right, it's all finished.'

'It looks good, Alan.'

'Well, be careful, you don't mess it all up. I'm not doing it again, OK?'

'Right, Alan.'

'The wide ones are the main roads, and obviously the narrow ones are the little roads.'

'What are them, then?'

'Dirt tracks. Can't you see they're separating the fields?'

'Where's the parking?'

'Right, I'm getting fed up. I won't have any time to play cricket. There's the parking, there's the garage space, there's where you change the speed limit, and there's the town centre. Now, don't bother me again. I need to concentrate on my cricket practice.'

These roadway maps, clearly etched on the cindery surface, enabled Keith to pass many happy hours. He filled the roads with his Dinky toys – motor cars, lorries, buses, agricultural vehicles, people, buildings, garages and all the rest of his equipment.

Ten yards away, completely undisturbed, I practised my cricket, hitting a tennis ball continually from bat to wall at varying speeds. I was glad when he was in my sight, because on the occasions that he wanted to play indoors, my practice would be interrupted.

'Listen, when the clock fingers are in this position, you come out and tell me you're all right.' The clock face was drawn on a page torn from one of my exercise books.

'Right, Alan.'

Quite often he forgot, which meant that these evenings were less pleasant.

'Right, count up to ten in French.'

'What, again?'

'Yes, if you can't remember simple instructions, you'll have to learn.'

'Un, deux, trois, quanter.'

Clip! Clip! Clip! CLIP! The "mistake" was always greeted with a heftier clip.

Even at his young age, then about six or seven, we had an understanding; when his mother was present, he knew he could ask for and have more or less anything he wanted, but when it was just him and me, he not only got nothing, he didn't dare ask. The moment my stepmother arrived home from her work, normally about eight o'clock, I went to bed.

Making Keith's breakfast was one of my biggest tests; it wasn't a difficult job, but it soon became my pet hate. I didn't bother to serve his meal with any pleasantness.

'Here.'

My stepmother was always watching. 'Put it over there. How many times do I have to tell you?'

Then, to Keith, 'Here you are, love, come and get your breakfast.'

'Can I have some more toast, mum?'

'Are you sure, love? You know you left some yesterday.'

'I'm hungry.'

'Get Keith another piece of toast, and don't burn it. What do you want to drink, love?'

Keith would be absorbed in his comic.

'Keith, love, do you want a cup of tea?'

'OK.'

'Bring Keith his tea. Don't spill it in the saucer.'

I went continually backwards and forwards in accordance with her demands and Keith's wishes. Sometimes I tried to annoy them. I enjoyed hearing Keith's complaining voice.

'I can't eat this, it's too burnt.'

'Mum, Alan's not put sugar in my tea.'

'Mum, there's no butter on my toast.'

If my stepmother was already in a bad mood, this added fuel to the fire and gave me some satisfaction.

While all this was going on, I ate my bread and jam standing up in the kitchen.

I usually sneaked a piece of toast and butter as well, or ate the discarded burnt toast.

'Before you disappear, bring a shovel of coal.'

'There's hardly any left.'

'Well put some coke in it, don't be stupid. Don't put it on the fire, leave it in the hearth. And listen, you better not have left that kitchen in a mess. It was like a pig sty yesterday.'

So, because of these changes in my home life, school homework suffered; often I was not even able to attempt it. A further constraint placed upon homework completion was the bedroom light. I was never allowed to disappear into my bedroom for any length of time if this meant switching on the light. Sometimes, the atmosphere in the living room was so threatening that my dark, cold bedroom was the only place to go. At bedtime, if I hadn't switched off the light after ten minutes, I heard her familiar unfriendly stomp up the stairs; then the light was switched off and the door noisily slammed shut. Lying in bed, I could see Keith's bedroom light shining dimly through the gap at the bottom of my door. His door was always left partially open and his light never switched off until my parents went to bed. Any objections from me at any time, for whatever reason proved fruitless. They were instantly dismissed and I was summarily dealt with, either by hand, a quick sharp clout, or by a raised warning voice, bellowing out words like, 'Get out of my sight!'

I never seemed to learn. Sometimes, unable to prevent myself, I would object. Breakfast time was usually when I weakened.

'I'm not doing this again. If you want your breakfast, get it yourself.'

'Don't ever speak to me like that.'

'I get the orange boxes, chop the firewood, make the fire, make your breakfast, make Keith's breakfast, you just sit there and he just looks at his comic. I'm not doing it again. Anyway, I could read at his age. He can't even read. He's stupid. I could read books at his age, never mind comics.'

My stepmother always swore when she was angry, and I was the one who usually made her angry.

'Stop it, you bloody cheeky bugger! Get out and take your bloody books with you!'

The result was always the same. I was thrust or pushed out of the open back door, followed by my dilapidated school satchel with its broken buckle fasteners. I often arrived at school hoping that, by the end of registration, my exercise books had dried sufficiently to look presentable, having been scattered over the backyard, which, in the winter, always seemed to be wet.

It was in one of those weaker moments, thrown out of the house for complaining, and trudging the two miles to school, that my mind once again drifted to my grandma's.

'Hello, Grandma, it's me again.'

'Eee, come in, Alan. Sit down on your grandad's chair. He's in his greenhouse, smoking his pipe.'

With a surge of intense relief, I sat down. My grandma was her usual busy self, but this just made everything more pleasant and peaceful.

'How are you getting on, Alan?'

'It's no good. It's getting worse. Grandma, you know I really liked my big school – I was tenth in class and picked for the football team.'

'Yes, you sounded really happy. After you left, your grandad said you'd soon be top of the class. He said you'd only got seven girls to beat.'

'Grandma, I need a miracle!' At that point I burst into tears.

'Oh, Alan, what's wrong? Why are you so sad?'

'They've moved house again. It's miles away from Wigan. I came home from school on Friday night and I was in another school on Monday. It's a rotten school. Nobody likes me. I don't know what to do.'

Just then, Grandad came in from his greenhouse.

'Eee, hello, lad. I see you've found the best chair in the house.'

'Alan's upset. They've moved house, and he can't settle in his new school.'

'Here's your chair, Grandad. I'll sit on the couch.'

'Thanks, lad. That's bad news. But listen, lad, you'll be all right when you show them how good you are at football, won't you?'

'They play rugby. I'm too small for that stupid game.'

'Eee, that's bad news, lad.'

'That's not all. Grandma, since we've moved, I've got to do loads of jobs and now I can't even do my homework.'

'What does your dad say?'

'Nothing. He just eats his tea and goes out to the club. Sometimes, I get fed up and I complain.'

'What happens? Do you get smacked?'

‘She sometimes gives me a clout, but it doesn’t hurt. She usually tells me to get out of her sight. My dad just tells me to get upstairs. What can I do?’

‘Well, first of all, let me give you a big spoonful of malt. Then we’ll have our tea and think about what to do.’

The truth was, they were stumbling in their attempts to find a solution. My grandma kept saying their hands were tied, and my grandad could only say that it was bad news. For the first time in my life, I wished I hadn't come to see my grandparents. I had upset them. I tried to repair the damage by appearing more cheerful than I really felt.

‘Grandma, I’m glad I came to see you. You’ve made me feel better – it's like having three big spoonfuls of malt.’

My grandad looked lost, so I explained. I reminded him of all the happy faces on the Golden Mile, and Grandma saying that it looked as if they’d all had a spoonful of malt. He now looked happy and so did my grandma.

‘Right, well, I’d better get going. When I get fed up or feel lonely, even if I’ve not got time to come and visit you, I’ll still think about you and ask for your help. Goodbye, Grandma, goodbye, Grandad.’

Now, feeling sad but also comforted, I could leave them; they had no solution, but just being in their presence had raised my spirits. I carried on walking to school.

# Papering over the Cracks

Surprisingly, I didn't often behave badly, despite being treated so unfairly. My response was an obstinate refusal to grow up. My mental and physical states lagged far behind those of my peers. For me, adolescence seemed endless.

The one experience that did have an instant effect on me was becoming a paper boy. I started delivering daily papers when I was twelve, and remained in the newspaper delivery trade in one form or another until I was eighteen. I delivered them in the morning between seven and eight, and in the evening between four and five, from when I was twelve until I was sixteen. I was often allowed the use of the paper bike for private purposes, which was a wonderful bonus to top up my wages of twelve and six a week. Not that I could keep all this; I was given two shillings, which never increased by one penny in all those four years. It is obvious that I had become very slow-witted. When living with my grandparents, I had been encouraged to use my brain, but since those days, I had plainly lost the technique. The newsagent always handed me a ten-shilling note and half a crown every Friday evening. I would then hand the full amount over to my stepmother.

'Here.'

'Right.'

'Can I have my pocket money?'

'I've no change. I'll give it to you later.'

Because on such occasions I sometimes would receive no pay at all, I began to complain.

'You don't always give me my two shillings. I deserve it.'

'Shut up. Don't tell me what you deserve. You don't know what it costs to feed and clothe you. That's where all the money goes, on you.'

‘What about all them cigarettes you smoke? You must have money to burn.’

‘Any more of your lip and you won’t get any pocket money at all. Go and get that shopping and hurry up. Your tea will be on the table.’ She would put out my meal when it was ready, even if I wasn’t there, so I often ate cold food.

I hadn’t got the gumption to ask the newsagent for a two shilling piece and a sixpence; that would have made it more difficult for my stepmother to keep the entire amount. It was months, probably a year, before this solution dawned on me.

However, I had the sense never to disclose my Christmas tips; because of my reliability and long service, these amounted to a good sum. In this instance, I did use my brain; my technique was to knock on every door to which I delivered, then smile and wish the owner of the house a Merry Christmas. This friendly approach was my pièce de résistance, and it generally worked.

‘Oh, hello, Alan. Just a minute.’

I then waited eagerly, wondering what would be the size of the tip offered as a thank-you for delivering their papers, morning and evening, six days each week for a whole year. Whatever I received, I was happy knowing that the whole Christmas tip collection would be a substantial sum.

‘Here you are, Alan. Merry Christmas, and thank you for bringing our papers.’

‘Thank you very much. Cheerio!’

‘Cheerio!’ sounded American. I always liked saying it.

If people happened to be out, I easily noted the number, and called back later that evening. Because the paper had already been delivered, I just had to say,

‘Hello, I’ve just called to say Merry Christmas.’

This approach always seemed to be successful; eventually, I had wished everyone on my paper round a Merry Christmas, being rewarded with a substantial response. The strange thing was that, despite my difficulties at home, the bulk of these Christmas tips ended up in the form of presents for my dad, stepmother and half-brother. The rest I would spend on cigarettes for myself.

I felt grown-up being a paper boy, now with a sense of being taller and stronger, sometimes running the entire round, using it as a training session for the cross-country.

The closest I ever came to falling into wicked ways was during these four years.

I thought of one of my grandma's maxims – 'Never bite the hand that feeds you.' My wages, twelve shillings and sixpence, reduced by two shillings, were not enough to feed us for a week, but were certainly, as my stepmother often reminded me, looked on as a necessity.

I suppose it all started with the freedom of having two shillings a week to spend. Under the threatening influence of two or three "Naughty Boys", I became involved in their furtive activities, and started buying cigarettes, usually Woodbines, Pasha or Compass, to hand out to them. It soon reached the point all my weekly two shillings were being spent on smoking.

Donald knew that I smoked.

'Will you lend me eightpence, Donald?'

'It depends. What for?'

'I want to buy five Woodbines and I've no money.'

'But you only smoke one a day and you're getting two shillings a week, so why have you got no money? You never go out. So where are you spending the rest of it?'

'I don't want a lecture, I just want eightpence.'

I didn't want to tell Donald that I was buying cigarettes for a corner street gang – he would never have given me money for that.

'Well listen, Alan, I'll lend you eightpence, but I think my grandma's right.'

'What do you mean?'

'Well, I don't think I'll get it back, and she always says, 'Once bitten, twice shy.' So here, go and buy your stupid fags, but don't ask me for any more money, OK?'

'OK, Donald. Thanks.'

That eightpence wasn't the only thing I borrowed. I even managed to add a few more cigarettes, expertly stolen from my dad's Player's twenty packet. I took them one at a time and hid them in my bedroom; by the time the weekly two shillings cigarette money was spent and smoked by the ever-grateful gang members, I would have accumulated several of these top-quality cigarettes, which were always greedily welcomed.

They stood on the street corners, smoking my cigarettes, swearing and laughing loudly at some crude joke. I felt trapped and uncomfortable. Because they frightened me, I would hand over the cigarettes and make an excuse to leave.

Occasionally, though, they encouraged me to stay.

'Right, I've got to go and look after my brother.'

'Forget him, kid. Here, have a light.'

'Oh, thanks.'

'You're doing well, kid, keep it up.'

'Do you know any good jokes, kid?'

'No.'

'Hang about with us and you'll soon know loads.'

'Listen, kid, start wearing long pants and we might let you join our gang, OK?'

'All right.' For once I didn't want to say OK.

'Right, kid, see you tomorrow night. Try and bring us some Players. I've not had one of them for ages. OK, kid?'

'All right.'

Because I usually made a quick getaway, and now feeling the need to smoke, I often secreted myself in an inconspicuous place on the railway embankment, sitting there with a cigarette, and thinking about my earlier life with my grandparents. Sometimes, knowing that I shouldn't be smoking, I would stub out a newly-lit cigarette, the pangs of guilt taking over. If I had been living with my grandparents, I wouldn't be doing all these wicked things.

This wickedness took hold; wanting more cigarettes, I looked for another source of supply. I didn't need to look very far. On the newsagent's counter, within easy reach, were packets of cigarettes, on display to attract customers. It was very easy for me to lean on the counter after my delivery was complete, pretend to be reading a comic and, when all was quiet, with the newsagent in the back room, grab a packet of ten cigarettes, which then magically vanished into my newspaper bag. It was common practice for me to take it home, so, once in the bag, the cigarettes were mine.

Over the next few weeks, I used this method to obtain cigarettes for the gang. For all the wrong reasons, I began to feel grown up. I knew I was doing wrong, but it all seemed so easy. What caused me the most concern was the gang. I was becoming even more frightened. What to do? Donald had always helped me when I was in trouble, so why not now?

My only chance to speak to him was at the kitchen sink.

'Donald, I'm in trouble.'

'Don't mention that word to me. I've got troubles every day. I wake –'

'But listen, Donald, mine's serious. I've been roped in with this gang.'

'What do you mean?'

'It's these three lads. They stand on the street corner smoking my cigarettes.'

'Well, don't give then any. It's simple.'

'It's not. I'll get bashed up. Donald, will you go and tell them? They only live in the next street. One of them is Tommy's brother.' Tommy was about Donald's age and I'd seen them together sometimes.

'Oh, sort it out yourself, Alan. I've not got time.'

'But I don't know what to do. There's three of them, and I'm scared of them. Listen, if you won't help me, will you ask Tommy to tell them to stop?'

'OK, I'll ask him when I see him. But I work in seconds, Alan – if the bus is a second early, I've missed it, and if it's a second late, I'm in a bad temper.'

So I went against my grandad's advice never to volunteer.

'What if I wash up the pots so that you'll have more time, then you'll be able to see Tommy?'

'That's a good idea. OK, you might as well start now.'

Because Donald was freed from washing up, I found it even more difficult to speak to him. 'We seek him here, we seek him there' – like the Scarlet Pimpernel, he was certainly elusive. If I managed to catch his eye, usually at teatime, he just shrugged his shoulders and looked away. Then I cornered him.

'I thought you were going to ask Tommy.'

'I've called for him three times. He's never in. I'll just have to keep trying.'

'Can you try your best? It's getting worse. Sometimes I'm scared stiff.'

'OK, but Tommy's like me, he wants to get out of the house. I'll try and find out where he goes.'

Shortly after this promise, when I had just swiped the usual ten cigarettes, and in the moment that they were vanishing into the bag, I saw this man peering through the newsagent's window.

He seemed to be looking straight at me and to have witnessed my action. I couldn't move. He lingered for a moment, then turned; two steps would take him to the door.

The door never opened.

I waited for what seemed like ages before moving. Terrified, I left the paper shop and went straight to the railway embankment, not to have a smoke, but to have a quiet place to talk to my grandparents.

'Er, Grandma, I've come to see you. I've been doing bad things. You would say they're wicked.'

'Eee, Alan, whatever you've done I'm sure it's not your fault. Come and sit down, and you can tell me all about it.'

'Will you not tell Grandad? I don't want him to know.'

'All right, Alan. He's just gone out to his greenhouse, so he won't be back for an hour at least. I won't tell him if you don't want me to.'

'Thanks, Grandma. I've joined a gang. They smoke, and they make me give them cigarettes. I've been spending all my pocket money, but that's not enough now, and I've started stealing cigarettes from the paper shop, and today I nearly got caught.'

'How did you nearly get caught?'

'I was just putting a packet of Compass in my bag and I saw this man looking straight at me. He was outside, looking through the window. Grandma, what if he'd come in the shop? Would they have sent me to prison? Oh, Grandma, can you help me?'

'Listen, Alan, very carefully.' She always said this when she was most serious. 'First of all, you must never steal any more cigarettes. Whatever that gang say, remember you mustn't do it anymore. Will you promise me that you won't steal any more cigarettes?'

'Yes, Grandma, I promise.'

'Well, that's settled. Now it's time for your spoonful of malt. You deserve it today – you've been very brave to tell me your troubles.'

'But what about that gang? I'm scared of them.'

'Eee, Alan, you're like a fish out of water. All I know is that if you're no use to them, they probably won't want you in their gang. But listen, don't argue with them, or you might get hurt. Just try and make them think you're no use to them.'

'Right, Grandma, I won't steal any more cigarettes, and the rest is up to me. Thanks, Grandma. I'll just go and see Grandad, then I'd better get going.'

'All right, Alan. And don't be worrying. I won't mention anything to him. And you leave that gang.'

I left the embankment with my mind made up.

From that day, I stopped stealing cigarettes. I managed to get away from the gang by finally starting to use my brains.

'These are the last ones.'

I had practised these lines repeatedly, but it didn't do me any good. They were probably the most difficult words I had ever had to speak.

'What do you mean, kid?' There were only two of them there. This one was the one who had seemed the most friendly, but now he suddenly looked menacing.

'I can't get any more.'

The other one joined in.

'Right, kid, what do you think you're on about? You better not be trying it on with us.'

'It's my mother. She's stopped giving me any paper money. She says she needs it out of necessity.'

'What the bloody hell are you talking about?'

'She won't give me any money, so I can't get any more cigarettes.'

'Did you hear that, Joe?' The third gang member had just arrived.

'Yeah, well, he's just a kid anyway. We don't want him in our gang. Bugger off, kid.'

That's when I escaped from the street corner gang, and that's when I thought, *Thanks, Grandma. Thanks for telling me what to do.*

I had never told Donald about stealing cigarettes, and in the end I was glad. I had put things right finally without his or Tommy's help. Of course, the washing up stopped immediately. This was decided at the tea table.

'Donald, when you wash up tonight, will you make sure the plates are clean?'

His face went red; he looked really angry. My parents didn't comment; in fact, nobody spoke. After tea, Donald didn't disappear.

‘What are you playing at, saying stupid things like that?’

‘Well, I never see you. How else can I start you washing up again?’

‘You can forget Tommy. I hope them three lads flatten you. That’s what I feel like doing.’

‘You don’t need to tell Tommy. I’ve sorted everything out myself. I just told them I’m not giving them any more cigarettes and then I just walked away. Like you said in the first place, it was simple.’

This implied praise helped to pacify him; his anger subsided and things returned to normal.

The entanglement in furtive activity had reached into my school life. I was befriended there and influenced by a “streetwise” boy. He knew all the tricks, including how to evade capture. This friendship started when he discovered I was his access to cigarettes. Suddenly, every dinnertime, I found myself cloistered with this boy, hidden in the furthest corner of one of the school’s general storerooms. We spent the time smoking cigarettes, mine, of course. It was always an extremely nerve-racking experience. It seemed to me that if we were caught smoking in that room, it would be definite grounds for expulsion. The room was opposite the staff room, which was out of bounds to pupils without official messages, so we had to be very wary. When the corridor was clear, one of us would slip into the storeroom and close the door, and moments later the other would enter. We then crawled or climbed into the furthest corner to smoke. On one such occasion, I was the first to sneak in, but the other boy never appeared. In those lonely few minutes, shaking and ill with fright, I realised the seriousness and stupidity of my actions. I managed somehow to pluck up enough courage to get out of the storeroom, but I wasn’t brave enough to end the dinnertime smoking relationship with this boy.

He hadn’t turned up that day because he had been caught and questioned, so, although he talked his way out of trouble, it was clear that we couldn’t use the storeroom again. He soon found another place, though, in the air-raid shelter in the corner of the school playing field, long abandoned and forgotten. The entrance was completely hidden by dense undergrowth, so we could sneak in easily without being spotted. Inside it was dark, dank and scary. I usually smoked with my eyes shut tightly, opening them occasionally to see my companion's contented face lit up in the glow of his, I mean my, cigarette.

I didn't like this boy, but didn't know how to escape from his clutches; luckily, once more, the liaison ended when the supply of cigarettes ceased.

These associations with the criminal element happened when I was thirteen and still wearing short trousers. Happily, realising that this life was not for me, I was relieved to escape its clutches. I had been, to quote Grandma, like a fish out of water, an innocent little boy trying to compete with rogues, and having nearly thrown in my lot with the naughty boys, was now glad to see them fade into the distance. I had made my choice, thanks to that man peering through the newsagent's window.

I never stole another cigarette, not even from my father's Player's packet.

Alas, I didn't stop smoking. For the rest of my school life, just over two years, I smoked secretly in my bedroom, in the dark, sitting very close to the empty fire grate so that I could blow the smoke up the chimney. The used matches and the extremely short cigarette stubs I poked up the chimney into the thickly soot-laden brick cavities. Even then, I knew smoking was a health hazard, especially to the likes of me, who found it difficult to breathe even in normal circumstances, but I already felt hooked, and needed my one cigarette a day.

Shortly after my escape from the criminal element, I finally progressed, in the fourth year, at fourteen years of age, to long trousers. Several boys, and quite a number of girls, commented on my sudden arrival into manhood.

'They make you look much older.'

'You can ask me for a date now you've grown up.'

'Oh, just look at this new boy – doesn't he look handsome.'

I felt glad to be wearing long trousers, but other than this superficial difference, there was no real change, mental or physical. However, it felt good to be noticed.

# It's a Dog's Life

There must have been a moment when Keith had a yearning to own a dog.

It involved me only when I was told to make a kennel.

'Go and get some orange boxes from the shop. It shouldn't take you long to make a kennel out of them.'

'What am I making a kennel for?'

'A dog.'

'Are we getting a dog?' I was now excited.

'We are getting a dog, but it doesn't come into the house. It stays in a kennel outside. So you'd better get it made quick.' My stepmother's tone was normal, but nevertheless I sensed that she didn't really want a dog.

So I set to work, fitting the kennel-making in with all my other chores. This, however, was a pleasant task. I spent one hour each day eagerly and happily sawing and hammering, until, after seven days, it was ready. It was quite a large kennel, about three feet square, with a pitched roof. I looked at it proudly, pleased with completing the task and happy with the result, even though it did look a little lopsided.

'The kennel's finished.'

'Right.'

Shortly after that terse acknowledgement of the completion of the work, a mongrel puppy arrived. I first set my eyes on it in the backyard on my arrival home from school. It had a black body and slightly overlong drooping ears flopping at the sides of an oval face. The little puppy moved awkwardly towards me, its body, including its chin, nervously brushing the ground, its wide black eyes frightened but appealing. I bent down and stroked it, then picked it up gently. This little puppy could be my friend.

'Leave that dog alone and come in here,' came my stepmother's impatient command.

Reluctantly, I walked into the kitchen.

'Go to the shop and get five pounds of potatoes and a loaf of bread.'

'Can I not get them after the papers? I'll be late if I don't go now.'

'Listen, don't give me your lip. If you hadn't been messing about with that dog, you wouldn't be late. Get going quick.'

She thrust the money into my hand and pushed me out of the house. As this was a normal welcome home, I should have been automatically resigned to such treatment, but today was different. Seeing that little black mongrel had made me excited, and was the cause of my foolish reaction in answering back.

I was never told the reason for the puppy being there; it was probably because of Keith's demands. However, his interest lasted only about a week. As his enthusiasm waned, mine strengthened to the point that I became the only one looking after him. I used to sneak him food, obtain a weekly bone from the local butcher, clean his kennel and take him for walks. I was the one who chose a name for him. For the next six months, Misty was my close companion.

I made a collar for him from an old piece of rope and used another for a lead. This enabled me to take him for walks and to have him accompany me when I went out to play at cricket or football. I tied his lead to a tree, occasionally running over to stroke him and play with him. He also ran the paper round with me, but this pleasure was soon stopped.

'Listen, Alan,' said the paper shop owner sternly. 'Come over here. I want to warn you about something.'

I was alarmed, because I had never seen him angry.

'Do you know what you've done?'

'No, what have I done?' I was frightened.

'You've let that dog destroy people's herbaceous plants.'

Luckily, I remembered the word "herbaceous" from working with my grandad, so I knew what he was accusing me of doing.

I couldn't deny it. Misty was difficult to control in confined spaces, and with my hands mainly occupied in posting the papers, he had trampled over the nearby border flowers.

‘I’m sorry. I won’t bring him again. Please let me still have a paper round. If you tell me who’s complained, I’ll knock on their door and apologise.’ I don’t know if it was these last few words that convinced him.

‘Right, Alan. I’ll be honest with you. Until this moment, I’ve never had a better paper lad. I believe you when you say you won’t bring your dog again. What I’ll do then is give you the four names and addresses, and you can go and apologise, then we can start from scratch.’ His tone was much calmer, and there had even been a hint of a smile as he spoke.

‘What does “start from scratch” mean?’ I was still not sure if I had a paper round.

The paper shop owner, now smiling, said, ‘Go home now with that dog, and then come back here for your papers. I’ll give you the addresses, and when you deliver their papers, you can knock on their doors and apologise. Then you start again being my best paper lad.’

Greatly relieved, I took Misty home, vowing to teach him some discipline. When I saw the border plants I was ashamed. I volunteered to tidy up the mess; all four people declined my offer, but accepted my apology.

The entire school summer holiday was spent trying, without success, to teach Misty the basic rudiments of self-discipline. It was, though, far from being a task. I looked forward to every day, rain or shine. I made up secret picnics, mainly of bread, margarine and jam, occasionally with a few broken biscuits, then off we would go, just the two of us, returning only in time for the evening papers. I spent hours throwing sticks or stones, in the faint hope, they would be returned, but the dog just ran anywhere and everywhere. Sometimes he would disappear; this always frightened me into thinking he had wandered off and got lost. Remarkably, considering his intelligence, this never happened. Either I would spot him frolicking in the distance like a little black sheep, or he would suddenly appear magically with his tail wagging furiously. I tried the ‘sit’, ‘lie down’, ‘wait’ and ‘heel’ commands endlessly throughout that summer, but to no avail. He always answered me by straining hard at the leash and yelping excitedly. The dismal failure to master these basics was the little dog’s downfall.

In those few short weeks he never did anything he was told, but if a dog ever had a master, then I was Misty's. He missed me when I wasn't there. In the early weeks, he showed this by whimpering and whining, then, later, by wailing and howling. In my absence, this was more or less continuous, all day and, worst of all, during the night; then I would slide the sash window quietly open and whisper hopeful pleas to try to coax him to stay silent. Of course, the moment I disappeared, the whimpering and whining started again.

The wailing and howling seemed to be limited to the daylight hours, and were welcoming sounds when I returned home from school, the noises stopping the instant I opened the back gate. This was the best moment of the day; it was a wonderful welcome home.

Then one day, as I crunched along the back street, I was met by an unusual silence. The wonder of this soon turned to worry, and before I had reached the back gate I was disconcerted to the point of panic. I ran and opened the gate frantically, only to find an empty kennel. I ran into the kitchen.

'Where's my dog?' I must have sounded hysterical.

'It's gone. The next-door neighbour's poisoned it. She kept threatening to do it. She said if we didn't stop it from making all that racket, she'd poison it. She couldn't get any peace. It was non-stop day and night.'

I don't know if my stepmother realised the state I was in, but she carried on anyway.

'I kept telling you to sort out that dog and stop its racket. It's your dog. If you can't control it, what do you expect?'

I ran out of the house screaming. Crying, I delivered the papers, then spent the rest of that awful day sobbing in my bedroom.

It wasn't long after this when I was told to chop up the kennel.

'It's not only an eyesore, it's a waste; chop it up for firewood.'

I never spoke to the neighbours again.

However, slow realisation has brought me to the firm belief that my parents' claiming that the neighbour had poisoned the dog was just a cover for the truth – my parents, perhaps because of complaining neighbours and their own inability to stop the continuous noise, had the dog taken away, to where I'll never know.

Several weeks after my little mongrel disappeared, another dog came on the scene. But this, as my grandma would say, was 'a different kettle of fish'. It was a Pekingese, a pedigree. Too good for a kennel, it lived in the house. Being my stepmother's dog, it had top priority and ruled the household. It took an instant dislike to me. I always had to give it a wide berth, or receive a torrent of grief in the form of ferocious, snappy yelps and vicious bites. When I arrived home from school, if the Pekingese was in the yard, I was frightened to open the gate. It snapped and snarled and bit at my ankles all the way to the kitchen door. Sometimes, the situation was such that I preferred to risk my stepmother's anger, and when the Pekingese went berserk, I defended myself with a swinging school satchel or a hopefully well-aimed kick. Quite often, I had to return to the backyard to retrieve school books that had come flying out of the broken satchel. It saddened me to remember Misty's very different welcome.

Inside the house, it strutted from room to room, curved tail resting on its back and head held high and proud. When I was left alone to baby-sit, I got Keith to put the dog into my parents' bedroom, and let it out just before they arrived home. In the mornings, luckily, when I was up and about doing my chores, the dog would appear only when my stepmother surfaced, and by then, I could get out of the way.

The situation never changed. When I went within two feet of that dog, especially if my stepmother wasn't in sight, it took a snap at me; strangely, it was less likely to snap if she was in the room, though I still kept my distance. Misty had been a friend – this dog was an enemy, and I was frightened of it.

Several years later, we moved house, and this Pekingese, to my intense relief, disappeared. This time there were no rumours of poisonings. It seemed to be "necessity" again. My parents' new plans saw both Keith and that Pekingese farmed out to one of my stepmother's relatives. As my grandma would say, every cloud has a silver lining.

# Pushed to the Limit

My dad was a heavily-built, stocky man with dark hair, brown eyes and a round, generally cheery face. He thought of himself as a singer, either a crooner like Bing Crosby or a tenor like Josef Locke. He often sat in his armchair by the coal fire singing "*Blue Skies*", "*White Christmas*", "*Galway Bay*", "*Violetta*", "*Killarney*" and the like. These few songs were his whole repertoire. I liked to hear him sing; it created a comforting atmosphere, and he looked different when he was singing. I would slow down working through my list of jobs to listen, and wait expectantly for the rendition to finish, usually on a sustained high note.

All he wanted was peace and quiet. After work, his usual timetable was to eat his meal, read the newspaper and nod off in his fireside chair; then after a wash and brush up, he would set off to the British Legion Club. During the years in Leyland, he became the secretary; if an excuse was needed to be out of the house, then this was it.

He stayed out of any argument for as long as possible. I was glad of this because he was blessed with a frighteningly large fist. This fist never touched me, but over thirteen years, it was often menacingly waved so close to my face that it called to my mind the phrase "within an inch of my life".

In the short space of one week in particular, I pushed my dad to the limit, and I was even more aware of this phrase. Two of his sayings were involved in this – "Up to your tricks", meaning I was up to no good, and "in't wires", which needs more explanation. This saying had become common in the first world war; if, when attacking, or retreating from an assault, you found yourself stuck in the barbed wirelines, then you were in trouble, a “sitting duck”, as my grandad said. So, “in’t wires” meant trouble, trouble that was very difficult to escape from.

It happened towards the end of the school summer holidays, just before I started wearing long trousers, when I was fourteen.

‘Your cousin is coming to stay for a week.’ My stepmother’s words didn’t register at first.

‘What do you mean?’

‘I mean your cousin is coming to stay, and you’d better be on your best behaviour. I don’t want any of your lip.’

‘Which cousin?’

‘Dennis.’ Dennis was my dad’s sister’s son. My face lit up. Dennis was two years younger than me, but since we’d been to the same junior school, we had regularly played together and were quite good friends.

He arrived the next day. It was like a holiday for me, suddenly freed from the bulk of my everyday chores. I didn’t even have to wash up. Dennis came on my morning and evening paper round, which I really enjoyed. Right from the start, we had a super time, happy just playing cricket and football.

It was the second evening of his stay when one of my grandma’s wise sayings – “sticks and stones will break my bones, but names will never hurt me” – was unwisely ignored.

Entering our street, feeling happy and planning the next day’s activities, I heard a sneering voice: ‘Here comes the puny kid. Skinny, skinny, skinny! He’s just a puny little skinny kid.’ This was bellowed out by a scowling tough-looking urchin, one of the smoking group that thankfully I had recently left. Whenever any of them saw me, they would call me names. Normally, I would ignore them, but on that evening, probably wanting to impress my cousin, I reacted differently.

‘I can still throw a ball further than you!’ I picked up his tennis ball and threw it with all my might down the street.

For a moment, he was taken by surprise, but soon recovered to shout his loudest.

‘You stupid fool! Go and get that ball, quick!’

‘Get it yourself. Come on, Dennis.’

‘I’ll get you, you skinny, puny kid,’ resounded in my head as we carried on down the street.

‘That was daft, Alan,’ said Dennis. ‘He’ll bash you up when I’ve gone home.’

‘No, he won’t, he’s soft.’ I was vaguely planning to steal a cigarette from my dad’s Player’s packet to pacify him.

The next evening, entering our street after another great day, I was grabbed, and had my arms pinned behind my back by two other members of the smoking group. The tennis ball kid directed proceedings.

‘Hold his hands behind his back. Right, that’s for throwing the ball down the street, and that’s for laughing at me, and that’s so you better not do it again.’ “That” each time was a solid blow to the stomach. Worse was to come. All three gang members lifted me and threw me over a front garden wall, where I fell heavily onto some very prickly roses.

Meanwhile, Dennis had disappeared, not running away, but going for help.

My dad showed his face in time to see me staggering down the street.

‘What happened?’ He sounded more annoyed than concerned.

‘Three lads thumped me. They’ve gone that way.’

I never thought my dad would do anything, but this time he did. He went off in the direction I’d shown, and returned shortly afterwards looking very pale, shaken and out of breath.

‘They said you threw his ball down the street and laughed at him. I thought it would be your own daft fault. Up to your stupid tricks again.’ He had struggled to speak these words, but he looked very angry, and I was glad that Dennis was standing next to me.

‘But, Uncle Bob, one of them lads started it. He was calling Alan names for no reason,’ said a surprised Dennis.

‘Well, just leave it. You’d better get in the house and get cleaned up.’

I was relieved that Dennis had spoken, because my dad wouldn’t have bothered to listen to me. As it was, he made no effort to console me or even comment on my battered condition, but, though he still looked angry, that seemed to be the end of the matter.

Towards the end of this eventful week, we planned to pinch some pears from a big garden overlooking the main road, near to where I lived. It was Dennis’s idea; every time we passed the orchard to go playing cricket or football, he would say how good the pears looked, though I didn't really need too much convincing.

'OK, Dennis, we'll get some.'

Clambering over the low stone wall was easy enough, but after numerous vain attempts to dislodge the pears we left empty-handed. But not defeated.

'Listen, Dennis, I've got an idea. I know where there's a ladder, then it'll be easy.'

'Eee, that's a good idea, Alan. Come on!'

Dennis's enthusiasm waned considerably, though, when he realised I was borrowing the ladder from somebody's backyard without bothering to ask.

'Come on, Dennis, it'll only be for half an hour, then we can take it back. It'll be worth it – look at all the pears we can get.'

After a bit more work, his resistance crumbled; we sneaked into the backyard, collected the ladder, quickly carried it the two hundred yards or so to the orchard, hauled it over the wall and across to the trees.

'Right, Dennis, I'll go up and throw them down. You can carry them in your pullover, OK?'

'OK. Hurry up before we're spotted.' He was scared.

Everything was going to plan, until, 'Hey! You two! What are you doing?'

We didn't stop. Dennis picked up the pullover, nearly full of pears, and ran. I jumped off the ladder, got up and followed him. About two hundred yards along the main road, we turned off, and thinking we were safe, stopped to share out the pears.

But almost immediately, a Land rover appeared. A man got out.

'You two – hop in the back. And bring those pears!'

We didn't argue. The short journey to the big house, undertaken in complete silence, was enough for us to become terrified. I could see my dad's look of contempt, and hear his words, 'You're in t'wires now, lad.'

We were ushered into a big kitchen.

'Right, where do you live?'

I found some courage from somewhere, and managed to speak, stammering out my address and explaining that my cousin was on holiday with us. Dennis never spoke.

'Right, you two. I can see you're not cheeky brats, so I'm going to let you off. And you can have two pears each for your trouble, OK?'

The reaction was simultaneous. 'Eee, thanks!'

'Right, get going – but don't come back!'

We went. We were so relieved that one important matter was completely forgotten.

The next day Dennis went back home. It had been a wonderful week, but things now returned to normal. I kept out of my dad's way in case he hadn't simmered down.

A few days later, the man from the big house paid us a visit. My dad opened the door.

'Have you lost your ladder?' the man asked.

'No, we haven't got one.'

'Ah, I'll need to explain.'

'Come in a minute, then,' my dad said.

This was when the man saw me. Once again I was terrified.

'Ah, this is the young man. A very polite young man he is too.' He must have realised I was heading for trouble, and was trying to soften the blow. 'All I wanted was for the ladder to be collected.'

My dad turned to me. 'What do you know about this ladder, then?'

'We used it to get some pears.'

'Pears?'

'Yes, Dennis wanted some before he went home.'

'So where did the ladder come from?'

'Mr Johnson's.'

'Did you ask him if you could borrow it?'

'No, he wasn't in.'

'So you just took it, did you? Right, go and get it, and give it him back.'

Carrying that ladder by myself those two hundred yards was a struggle, especially with the thought that I still had to face Mr Johnson.

He opened his front door.

'Hello, Mr Johnson. I've brought your ladder back.'

He looked puzzled. 'What do you mean, you've brought my ladder back?'

'I borrowed it to climb up a tree. You weren't in, and my cousin was going home the next day so we had to get the pears that day and you were the only person I knew with a ladder.'

I waited anxiously for his reaction. He seemed even more puzzled.

'Right, then. Take it round the back and put it where you found it. But listen, Alan, don't take it again without asking me first, will you?'

'OK, Mr Johnson. I'm sorry, and I won't take it again.' I certainly wouldn't go through all this again for the sake of a couple of pears, I knew that.

I hoped that was the end of it, but I should have known better. When I reached home, my dad was waiting for me. He was fuming. His fist came towards my face.

'You stupid, daft fool! Up to your stupid, daft tricks again! You've had me running like a madman down the street, chasing after some innocent kid, you've had people knocking on my door telling me you've been in gardens pinching pears, then I find you're entering private property and stealing ladders. You're supposed to be on holiday with your cousin, and all you're doing is causing trouble. The more I do for you, the more stupid you get.'

All through this, I was steadily inching backwards to get away from that big fist, which was moving closer to my face with every word. It had never been so close. It filled my vision. If I had any thought of being cheeky and telling him he didn't know the difference between singular and plural – it had been only one man and only one garden – that fist certainly stopped me.

Then, welcome words – 'Get to your room! Get out of my sight!' I disappeared, very quickly.

# Be Prepared

Life at home was still affecting school and holding me back. My daily timetable never altered during those final two years; I had jobs to do before and after school.

Before school, I had to clean out the fire grate and prepare the fire for lighting, deliver the morning papers, then light the fire and make Keith's breakfast, having my own while doing the last two jobs. Only after all this, could I leave.

After school I delivered the evening papers, cleared the table after tea, washed the pots, and then looked after Keith, fitting in any other jobs, such as filling the coal scuttle, chopping firewood, and hanging out or bringing in washing.

Not surprisingly, I rarely attempted my homework, especially in the winter months, usually copying it from someone during morning registration. My attitude remained silly, and the outlook seemed hopeless. The GCE examination was a distant dream. I was only a little boy, still fighting in some form or other against all the confusion of this second life. But something must have stayed with me from my first life. The GCE qualification, even I realised, was important. My father had already warned me of this when he described my probable future:

'Get them GCEs or you'll end up sweeping the streets.'

'How do you expect me to learn when I can't even do my homework?'

'You've learned how to be cheeky. Just get them GCEs.'

This was a typical futile attempt to stand up for myself, usually getting no further than one sentence.

I felt I was heading for trouble, and the lack of GCEs would be the cause of it. My main strength in times like this would be my grandparents. So once again my imagination took me up that unevenly-flagged garden path, through the front door, along the lobby and into the sitting room.

'Hello, Grandma, hello, Grandad.'

'Eee, come on, lad, sit yourself down.' Grandad reached for his pipe.

'What's wrong, Alan? You look upset.' My grandma always seemed to know how I was feeling. I had long ago realised there was no fooling her.

'It's my GCEs. I'm not as clever as I used to be, but I need to get them.'

'Why? It's only a piece of paper,' said Grandad, sounding clever.

'But it'll help to stop me brushing the streets.'

'Well, Alan, it's better late than never,' said Grandma.

'Polly, put the kettle on, and me and Alan will think of a plan.'

As she went into the kitchen, I turned to him. 'What can I do, Grandad?' After several thoughtful puffs, he came up with his answer.

'You can do your best, lad. If you do your best, you've done enough.'

I was happy in my grandparents' company. They always tried to help me; their advice was never complicated, and their simple words were a great comfort to me. I was now able to think of the looming GCE exams much more calmly.

I looked at all my school subjects, analysed each one, and after working out all the probable failures, asked myself, would I be prepared for the consequences. The lighter evenings gave me a glimmer of hope. I had only a few weeks, but nevertheless this provided the opportunity for some covert exam preparation after eight o'clock. It wasn't revision, because I had never learned in the first place. In certain subjects, my level of understanding was so weak that I struggled unsuccessfully to grasp the fundamentals. Not surprisingly, the three subjects in which I finally attained GCE level fitted in with my three-factor analysis:

History – Pass (frightened of the teacher)

Geography – Pass (liked the teacher)

English Language – Pass (liked the teacher)

Two other subjects I must have been very close to passing were French and Woodwork. In both of these, I liked not only the teacher but also the subject, and they were the two I confidently felt I had passed. When the letter containing the GCE results arrived, it was hard to believe that they had not made a mistake. Then I realised that five GCEs would have been a miracle – especially when the three I did pass were three more than my final school report had forecast.

My dad came home from work and read the letter confirming my limited success. This time I wasn't dismissed with the money to go and buy cigarettes; he read the letter, placed it back on the dining table and, as he sat down to his evening meal, mumbled, 'Well, I suppose it wasn't a sheer waste of time.'

# Growing Pains

I left school but wasn't given a brush to sweep the streets.

I "saw" my grandparents to ask for their help with my GCEs. This was my last such "visit". I was still a very young sixteen, hardly embarked on the journey of adolescence. I had always been a silly pest in school and a badly mistreated skivvy in the house; in these circumstances, I had needed my grandparents. But after finishing school, my life began to change. I became more accepted in the house, and my leisure activities were widening; it was all new and all good. There were still moments when I would wonder if my grandparents would approve of my activities, but once at work, I never felt it necessary to go and "see" them.

I started work serving an apprenticeship at Leyland Motors. Part of the initiation was to have a simple form of medical, including height, weight, previous ailments, allergies and so on. When I started my apprenticeship, I was only four feet nine inches tall and six stone seven pounds in weight. This didn't worry me. But now I had been thrust into a completely different environment.

Everything seemed violent. I was surrounded by the constant deafening noise of the belt-driven motors operating line after line of machines, for gear-cutting, turning, shaping and drilling, and by an alarming number of working men, releasing their frustrated tensions in the form of raucous and sometimes uncouth behaviour. No longer able to hide behind the childish bravado of a schoolboy, I changed instantly from being silly to becoming timorous. School had been where I acted the clown to hide many of my self-doubts, but in the early months of this new working life, with all its unfamiliarity, I actually became frightened and very easily alarmed.

Ironically, for the first time in eight years, I was more relaxed at home than anywhere else. Maybe it was because nothing there had really changed.

It was the local custom that, as a gesture of growing independence, any boy starting his first job would be allowed to keep all of his first pay packet. Queuing up on the day of my first wage packet at Leyland Motors, I felt on top of the world. The amount written very clearly on the envelope was £2 3s 9d. As I arrived home, I was excited and felt grown up. My stepmother was making the tea.

'I've got my wage!'

'I hope you've not opened it.'

'No, I haven't. The amount's written on the front.'

'Well, come on then, give it here.'

'Can I not keep it? It's my first one. Everybody else is keeping theirs.'

'Well, you're not. You can start as you'll be carrying on. Come on, give it to me.'

I handed over my pay packet.

'Right, listen. You're getting a raise from two shillings to five shillings a week. That's more than enough.'

I had half expected this to happen; it was no use arguing, and anyway, I knew it wouldn't be too difficult to start adding to this meagre amount from other sources.

As Grandma would say, where there's a will there's a way.

I was given a further shilling a day to buy my dinner; I bought a daily meat and potato pie for sixpence, and so saved two and sixpence a week.

I had retired from my weekday paper round, so now, between six and seven in the morning, two days a week, I prepared the deliveries for the young lads, which gave me a further four shillings.

A Sunday morning paper round brought another four shillings.

In this way, I increased my weekly income from five shillings to fifteen and six, meaning that I worked all week at Leyland Motors for five shillings, and then for about four hours on part-time jobs to earn more than twice this amount.

The Sunday source of income sometimes clashed with the weekly visit to church. For whatever reason, only Heaven knows, my dad's main insistence had always been for me to continue at Sunday School. This is one thing I didn't resist; in fact, I wanted to go. I had never missed Sunday School when I was living with my grandparents, and didn't want to miss it after I had been taken away from them, so whatever my dad's reason was, I was glad.

My time at Sunday School did come to an end when, having moved to Leyland at twelve years old, I progressed to Sunday morning church service. I was never an altar boy, I just went to church. My dad still expected me to attend, although I went willingly, as the Sunday morning visit had become part of my life. I fitted in the church service at seven or eight o'clock in the morning, going on from there to deliver the Sunday papers. If I missed the morning service, I attended in the evening.

So I started working full-time at Leyland Motors. At first, this didn't affect my jobs in the home. I was still setting and clearing tables, preparing vegetables, washing up, cleaning windows, polishing and dusting, making fires, chopping wood, shopping on Saturday, collecting coke from the gasworks, collecting orange boxes for firewood and mangling, hanging out and folding washing. These continual demands on my time had always meant that opportunities for playing out were very limited, making it extremely difficult for me to make real friends. Playing with other children was always fun, but because of my unreliability as to when or for how long I could play out, I never made any best friends. By the time I was sixteen, and just starting work, I was one of those who knew everybody in the locality but was also, as Paul Anka would sing in his hit song several years further down the line, 'Just a lonely boy, lonely and blue.'

When I left school, it got worse. I very soon began to feel trapped; a skivvy in the house, a frightened boy at work and a lonely youth in the streets at night. One evening at tea, more downcast than usual, I blurted out my feelings.

'I've had enough of this. I do everything in this house.'

Both of my parents were startled. My stepmother was the first to react.

'What are you talking about?'

'I mean I do everything in this house. It can't be any clearer than that. All you do is shout and bawl at me.' I directed my gaze towards my dad. 'You don't know what goes on in this house. I do job after job and then get shoved out of the room. It's stupid. She's stupid. I've had enough.'

'Don't call me stupid, you cheeky bugger. If you don't shut your lip, I'll –' Crash!

My dad's fist hit the dining table.

'Shut up, both of you! I don't blame you, Alan. Now you've started work, things will have to change.'

At this point, my stepmother left the table, left the room, then moments later, left the house, slamming the front door shut behind her. Excitingly, it seemed in that moment she had left the house for ever. Never before had my dad taken my side in an argument. It wasn't, however, a sign of the future. He would never again speak out in my defence.

When the front door slammed, I looked triumphantly towards my dad, who was now slumped in his armchair, staring at the floor.

'Well,' I said, 'she's gone.'

'Oh, just get out of my sight. Get to your room, and quick. I've had enough of this. I don't want this after I've been working all bloody day.'

Nothing more was said, but my outburst did work in my favour. From that moment, changes began to creep into my home life. I now no longer looked after Keith on weekday evenings; this task was narrowed down to Saturday and Sunday evenings. I was also allowed to stay out on weekdays until half past eight, then to be in bed by nine o'clock. Those were the two major beneficial changes. Most of the other demands were still enforced in some form or other, but now there was greater flexibility.

Staying out to 8:30 often saw me showing off in front of the younger element in the local streets, then hiding furtively in some isolated area to smoke a cigarette. The boys of my age had now disappeared from these streets; many of them were chasing girls. Their absence meant that I had top status; there was no one left who could beat me. Nevertheless, my showing off was accompanied more and more by vague feelings of inadequacy. My days were spent working with men, listening to their, sometimes lewd, tales of long ago conquests, and with boys of my age, hearing about their previous night's experiences. In the evenings, I was showing off in front of ten-year-olds. Something needed to change.

I felt no desire to join in with the chase-the-girl activities, but something had to be done about these evenings. So I went to the local pub. It was easy to walk in and go straight up to the bar, because for six days a week over four years, I had walked the same steps, delivering the evening papers. But now I had a different reason for being there.

'Hello, Mr Blackmore. I've started work now.'

'I know you have, lad. That new newspaper lad's useless. Now then, what can I do for you?'

'Well, you said about going upstairs.'

'Yes, I did. That was two years ago – I didn't think you'd remember. Well, seeing as I promised, I'd better let you start, eh?'

'Thanks, Mr Blackmore!'

'Right, let me explain a few things. First, and most important, don't drop any weights, big or small, onto the floor. Place them, don't drop them. If you drop them, I'll know' – he pointed to the ceiling above his head – 'and you'll be straight out of the door. Second – and this is sound advice, lad – don't start showing off with heavy weights. If you want to build yourself up, just use light weights. Do you know what bulk means?'

'Plenty?'

'Well, in weightlifting terms, you get bulk from lifting heavy weights, and let me tell you, lad, bulk means fat. I'm telling you from experience. Just look at me – bulk means fat.'

I had always thought of Mr Blackmore as big, powerful and strong, not fat.

Thinking, though, that it would be unwise to agree with him, I asked him a question.

'What about the light weights? What do you get from them?'

'Definition, lad. Do you know what definition means?'

'Real?'

'Nearly right. Your muscles will be real because they won't be fat. Listen, I'll have a word with John and tell him to set you working on a basic definition programme – light weights and plenty of repetition. How often will you be training?'

'Can I come twice a week?'

‘That’s fine, lad. It’s a shilling a night and you can pay me at the bar before you go upstairs. Are you clear on everything?’

‘Yes, I think so. Can I start now? I’ve got a shilling.’

‘Right, off you go, then. Straight upstairs, right at the first landing and it’s the door facing you. John’s already up there. Tell him I want to see him.’

‘Thanks, Mr Blackmore.’

So Mr Blackmore kept his word, and twice or three times a week for the next eighteen months, I was in the room above the bar with two or three boys slightly older than me, following a weight training course designed by Mr Blackmore and improved by ourselves with help from Mr Universe monthly magazine. Strictly following Mr Blackmore’s sound advice, most of the time I was working to achieve muscular definition, by using light weights faster and more repetitively.

I had two weaknesses. I felt it very necessary to check frequently on my strengths with regard to two bulk lifts, the Dead Lift and the Standing Press. The training days went by with me trying to achieve heavier weights on these one-off lifts. The maximum I reached in the dead lift, with my arms hanging down completely straight and my shoulders straight back, was 200 lbs – double my bodyweight, now over seven stones. In the standing press, the objective was to dead lift the weight, and then, with both feet shoulder-width apart and perfectly still, reverse curl the weight to chest and shoulder level with no foot movement, then press upwards until the elbows locked in a straight line position with the weight high above the head. In this, I reached my target of 112 lbs, inspired by Grandma’s coalman and his hundredweight bags of coal.

So, two or three times a week, paying a shilling for each two-hour session, I was off the streets and beginning to feel good. I began to see muscle instead of bone. My self-confidence was improving, and this was helping me to feel more settled in both working atmosphere and home life.

At home, I was still hardly ever greeted or acknowledged by my first name, but the snappiness and curtness, and the continual feeling of being threatened had been replaced by a resigned acceptance in recognition of my growing up. There was no love or kindness in the real sense of the word, but the atmosphere was certainly more amiable. I had accepted my lot, but always with the hope that things would change for the better, and now they had. I was able to speak more than one sentence without being dismissed out of hand. Many of the jobs that had once been forcibly inflicted on me, I now did voluntarily; instead of 'Do this! Do that! Or else!' my stepmother now introduced jobs into the conversation at some relevant moment.

'At some point, we'll have to get…' This approach covered not only shopping items but jobs around the house.

'It'll look much better when it's done.' This usually related to a weekly job like polishing brasses or furniture, or cleaning windows.

'I've just got back from the shop and I haven't started setting the table or getting the tea ready.' So I set the table…

I usually ended up doing most of these jobs but felt now that I was helping out voluntarily.

Having reached seventeen years of age and negotiated a Friday night stay out until 9:30, I took the plunge, and walked very nervously, for the first time, into the town centre youth club. The voice of Tennessee Ernie Ford singing his hit song *Sixteen Tons* created a vibrant, welcoming atmosphere. The room was large, about as long as a cricket pitch and nearly the same in width. It was filled with fifteen to eighteen-year-old boys and girls, every one looking happy. I felt out of place, the urge to escape quickly overcoming Tennessee Ernie's initial welcome.

My eyes were drawn to the corner of the room, the one furthest from the entrance, or, more pertinently for me, the exit. In this far corner was a table tennis table. Still very nervous, but now attracted towards this distant corner, I passed along the main floor area; the diagonal approach across the crowded room was impossible, so with head slightly lowered, I inched myself along the side, occasionally looking up to see the faces of the dancing boys and girls. Many of them were holding each other tightly and seemed, from the looks on their faces, to have moved into another world. One or two of the boys, on spotting me looking, raised their eyebrows to me in acknowledgement of their conquest. When my eyes met a girl's, she would smile, making me feel funny. Creeping along, I mentally rejected any future involvement with the main floor, and in this scared and stumbling fashion, I eventually found my way to the table tennis corner.

‘Do you want a game?’

This friendly inquiry came from a ginger-haired boy who seemed to be a foot taller than me.

‘Well, this is the first time I’ve ever been to a youth club, and I’ve never played before, but I’d like to try.’

‘Right, come on, then. I’ll show you what to do. My name’s Bobby.’

‘My name’s Alan.’

‘Right, Alan, you have to hit the ball over the net so that it lands on my side of the table, then we keep hitting it back to each other. If I miss the ball, or miss your side of the table, you score a point. It’s the first to reach twenty-one. It’s easy, you’ll soon pick it up.’

‘Sounds a bit complicated.’

‘Let’s just practise hitting the ball to each other, and you’ll soon learn.’

‘OK, Bobby, thanks.’

‘That’s OK. If you like playing, we can have a game every week.’

This was a wonderful welcome.

I settled immediately into my Friday evening social activity. On that first evening, and on most of the other Fridays, my enjoyment centred on the table tennis table. During all those visits to the youth club, I never once used the pinball machine, which was in the area where the “borderline” boys would congregate. Neither did I ever ask a girl to dance; in fact, I don’t remember ever speaking to a girl. I just played table tennis.

Then there was my first holiday. Four of us seventeen-year-old boys were going to spend a week at Butlin’s. We were a group who never argued, but they couldn’t really understand my idea of what constituted a “great time”. This was a key moment in my teenage life. At seventeen, I looked no older than a very young looking fifteen. I would never be allowed in the Pig and Whistle in a month of Sundays. The other three boys were the opposite; they had no problems posing as eighteen-year-olds. If I had joined in with their idea of a good time on this holiday, I would have had a week completely out of my depth, but the new experience might have influenced me enough to want it to continue afterwards.

The Saturday finally arrived, and we found ourselves settling into our chalet.

'We'll have to have a timetable.' This was Brian; if there was a leader, he was the one.

'I don't need one. I know what I'm going to do,' said Tony.

'What?'

'I'm going to get up late, go to the Pig and Whistle, sunbathe, might have a swim, get ready for the night, go to the Pig and Whistle again and look for a woman.'

'Me as well,' Vinnie said.

'Well, that's settled,' Brian agreed. 'Isn't it great being away from that bloody noise?'

'Yeah, and I've not got Pinder watching me all the bloody time,' Vinnie added.

'Forget work,' said Tony. 'Let's just see how the other half live for a week. What about you, Alan? Are you going to chance it? You can sneak in between us so the Bluecoats won't spot you. Once we're in, you'll be OK.'

'I'm not bothered about having a drink, but I've got a timetable.'

'What is it?'

'I'm going to learn how to play table tennis. They've got coaching lessons twice a day with an England player, and then I can practise. And I want to learn how to play snooker and I can practise that by myself.'

'What about coming dancing with us?' asked Vinnie. 'We can all pick up a girl and bring them back here. Bloody hell, I can't wait.'

'I think I'll just practise my snooker, Vinnie. But I'll come sunbathing.'

'I can't think why you bothered to come to Butlin's,' said Brian.

'Well, you're my friends, and I was glad when you asked me to come. I won't be in your way, Brian. I'll play table tennis and snooker, and we'll all have a good time.'

'Well, that's settled. Let's see what the Pig and Whistle's like.'

My entire week was spent playing snooker or table tennis. Butlin's was the perfect place. I took up the wonderful opportunity to be coached by an ex-England table tennis player, practising hard and hopefully seeing results in the form of improving skills. Snooker, on the other hand, was a completely new game to me, and I quickly realised how skilful Joe Davis must have been. I could hardly pot a ball, but as snooker can be easily played alone, my time was spent trying to improve my game in comparative secrecy.

The other three boys were following their idea of having a great time, this being the freedom to drink and to enjoy the alluring fascination of strange girls.

Whenever I returned to the chalet during the day, one, two or all three of them would be on their beds, cuddling close to a girl. This was essentially their week: in the chalet, in the bar, in the dance hall, and always with a girl, usually a different one each day. I just remained oblivious to all that went on, and without the remotest resentment, disappeared back to my own world. It was just wonderful to feel the freedom snooker and table tennis provided. It was also a relief to be away for a whole week from all my tasks.

I returned home feeling like a hero. On the front page of the evening paper, in the bottom right hand corner, was a picture of me holding a table tennis bat in a "smash" pose. Beneath the picture were a few sentences commenting on my interest and potential. In those brief moments, I could have run a four-minute mile. Alas, no one else seemed bothered, and within a day of returning to work, everything had returned to normal.

Another activity which kept me off the streets and helped to put a stop to my showing off to the younger generation was cricket. I loved the game. The first thing I did after receiving my newspaper bag, full of the evening papers, was to look in the stop press for the latest county cricket scores; I would look for the close of play scores in the morning papers. When England were playing, there would be a commentary broadcast on the wireless. My favourite commentator was John Arlott; he made everything about cricket sound the way it should be, calm, peaceful, interesting and exciting. Sometimes on warm sunny days during school holidays, I stood quietly near someone's open door listening to him.

I had learned at an early age of the intense cricketing rivalry between Lancashire and Yorkshire, always referred to as the Battle of the Roses. This rivalry spilled over into Test cricket.

Even at Test level, for me, despite players being on the same England side, Lancashire would play Yorkshire when the opening batsmen happened to be Cyril Washbrook and Len Hutton and the bowlers Brian Statham and Fred Trueman.

My own playing prowess was limited to lower grade cricket. The engineering works had three teams. The first team competed at quite a high level, in the Northern League, where it wasn't uncommon for teams to field a professional who had played or was still playing for his country. The second team played at a distinctly lower level, so if ever a player stepped up from the second eleven to the first, he could end up being, as my grandma said, like a fish out of water. The first team was always far beyond my reach, but I did have dreams of cementing a permanent place in the second eleven.

The third team played their cricket at a much lower level than the second eleven; the team was selected, and hopefully all eleven players turned up on the evening of the match. I always turned up. I played for them as a leg break and googly bowler. At that level, I could bamboozle almost anyone, and regularly took match figures of five or more wickets with very few runs against, once getting seven wickets for only five runs. These fine analyses, along with my regular attendance at net practice two evenings each week, brought me to the notice of the second eleven captain, Mr Howard.

'Let's see how your googly's getting on.'

'Should I just bowl googlies?'

'Bowl me six balls, four leg breaks and two googlies. Mix them up.'

'Right, I'll try.'

'OK, I'm putting this bowling mat where you should pitch the ball. Keep trying to land the ball on the mat, OK?'

'Right. Should I keep bowling googlies?'

'Yes, mix them up, but keep them on the mat.'

This was a typical cricket practice under the charge of the captain.

'Right, Alan, now try and bowl faster. Don't just use your arm, try and use your body weight, especially the shoulder turn. I can't spot your googly, and you bowl a good length. If you can speed up, you'll make a good bowler.'

'Oh, thanks, Mr Howard.' It was good to hear praise and encouragement.

'Righto, Alan. Well, keep practising and I'll see how you're getting on next week. When you speed up a bit, I'll introduce you to the top spin. You'll get plenty of LBWs with top spinners. Good luck in the match this week.'

'Thanks, Mr Howard.'

I loved cricket, whatever the standard, but I was desperate to improve my game. I tried my very best, but my height and weight proved to be a severe handicap in moving up from thirds to seconds, although my skill was always acknowledged.

'I wouldn't believe it, if I hadn't seen it,' might be a comment on me spinning a leg break an extraordinary distance.

'I couldn't spot the difference,' after my bowling a googly and deceiving the batsman into thinking it was a leg break.

But I hadn't the physique to increase the speed of the ball through the air. Even for the second eleven, I wasn't equipped to compete. Nevertheless, I still attained second eleven status several times, usually when someone was ill. I became the ever-reliable first reserve, managing, in total, seven wickets for middling runs, being brought on to bowl when, in the captain's opinion, 'We can afford to lose a few runs.' These occasional appearances for the second eleven were restricted to home games, as I was needed at home on Saturday nights.

Even though I had turned eighteen, I had to babysit on Saturday and Sunday nights. Now, though, there was no strange babysitter, no shivering in the dark motor car, no sobbing myself to sleep; now I was in demand, now I was the babysitter. The baby was my half-brother, Keith, ten years old. My parents left me with the reminder: 'Don't forget to be in bed by nine o'clock.' I took advantage during these babysitting duties of the opportunity to smoke my cigarettes in the luxury of the sitting room, rather than hunched over the upstairs fire grate, blowing the smoke up the soot-laden chimney.

Although always in bed before my parents arrived home, I also took advantage of the newly-acquired television set, a Sobel with a fourteen-inch screen. My favourite programme was *Armchair Theatre* on Sunday nights. So, despite being restricted, I had some scope to develop further my weekend independence. On weekdays, I now felt totally independent, being involved in enjoyable activities which monopolised all my spare time, and which had finally helped me to escape from the streets and the company of ten-year-olds.

# Donald

Donald seemed to me to have achieved total independence. When he arrived in Leyland he was four years older than me in age but years ahead in everything else. At sixteen, all he had to do was wash up and then disappear. Days at a time passed and I didn't see him at all, and when he did appear it was only briefly.

'Hello, Alan.'

'Hello, Donald. Are you going out again?'

'Yes. The bus is in fifteen minutes. I'll have to get going. See you.'

In truth, we hardly spoke to each other, because we had little in common. One day, however, he surprised me. It was just about the time when I negotiated my first Friday night out to the youth club, a few weeks before he left home again, this time more or less for good. He sounded unusually happy.

'Hooray! I'll soon be leaving!'

'What do you mean? You're never here anyway, so it won't make any difference.'

'Well, I lead a busy life. What with my girlfriend and studying, I've no time for anything else.'

'What do you mean, studying? I've never seen you looking at a book.'

'Where can you study in this house? I'll tell you what, Alan, when I leave, it'll be the best day of my life.'

'Where do you study, then?' Had I missed an opportunity when I was trying to study for my GCEs?

'I go to my girlfriend's. It's brilliant. That's where I stay sometimes. Her parents really like me.'

Donald had been courting a girl from Chorley for nearly four years. I had never seen her. My not knowing about his studying and not having met his girlfriend showed how far we had grown apart. He didn't help me with any jobs, and although he had short conversations with our parents, apart from mealtimes, I never saw him sitting down. Ever since he had come back to live in our house, he just seemed to rush in from work, have his tea, wash up, get changed and dash away. 'I'm in a hurry,' he would say, 'I've got to get changed. I'll have to be quick, the bus is due.' Then he would make his getaway.

'Where are you going? Are you going to live at your girlfriend's?'

'No, I'm due for call up. I'll soon be joining the RAF. Two years away from this place – I can't wait.'

'But what about your girlfriend?'

'Well, listen, nobody knows yet, but we're going to get engaged, so when I come out of the RAF we can get married. Don't tell them. I'll tell them later.'

'All right, Donald, I won't, but I might tell them you think they're stupid.'

'Wait till I leave and you can tell them what you want.'

'You seem to have everything planned.'

'That's what you've got to do, Alan. It's the only way if you want to get on. Plan and study, that's what you've got to do.'

'What about your girlfriend? Is she included in your plans? Do you have time to study her?'

'She's what I call a distraction. But it's nice. When you've got a girlfriend, you'll know what I mean.'

Two or three weeks later, after officially announcing his engagement, he took me by surprise.

'Do you want to come and see my girlfriend?

'What do you mean?' This was my usual reaction to being surprised.

'I'd just like you to see my girlfriend and her parents before I join the RAF, and I'll be going soon.'

'OK. When?'

'This Sunday. If I'm not here on Saturday night, I'll come back home on Sunday.

You be ready at twelve o'clock, then we can go straight out.'

'OK. I'll go to church and take the papers, and I'll be ready. Listen, will you ask them if I can go? If I ask we'll only start arguing.'

'I've already asked them. They said it was all right. Well, my dad did; she just kept quiet.'

That Sunday was great. Donald's girlfriend was nice; she was very friendly and her parents were kind and welcoming. I was on my best behaviour, especially when we all sat down to tea. After tea, I felt more relaxed. Donald took me up to his girlfriend's room.

'This is where I spend all my time. I do my studying here.' I heard his girlfriend giggling.

'What's that?'

'It's a transistor radio.'

'What's a transistor?'

'It's just a wireless. We can listen to Radio Luxembourg?'

'What's that?'

'They play the top ten at seven o'clock.'

'What's the top ten?'

'It's all the best songs. Eee, Alan, do you not know anything? We'll listen tonight. It's great.'

'Will you not forget?'

'No. What else is there to do on a Sunday night?' More giggling.

So that evening I heard, for the first time, the latest pop songs played over the radio, and returned home feeling more grown up, yet wishing I was four years older. Donald was the epitome of total independence.

Shortly afterwards, he left. The finality of his leaving brought sadness for me. I didn't see him at all for the next two years. Soon after he was called up, a letter must have arrived.

'Well,' my dad said, 'your brother's not getting married after all.'

'Why not?'

'She won't change.'

'Change what?'

'Change her religion. She's a Roman Catholic and we're Church of England'

'Does it make a difference?'

'Yes, it makes a big difference.'

'But Donald's not that bothered about going to church.'

'Well, he's Church of England and that's it.'

'It won't make any difference to me what I am.'

'Listen, while you're in this house, you're Church of England and you go to church every Sunday.'

'It still won't make any difference.'

'Oh, just shut up, will you? You argue about everything. I'm just telling you Donald's got some sense. He's not getting married because she's a Roman Catholic and we're Church of England, and that's it.'

Donald must have been very upset after the breakup, which caused him to drink quite heavily. He was brought to his senses when one Saturday night in Weston Super Mare, his local town to RAF Locking, he was knocked unconscious in a drunken brawl and spent some time in hospital suffering from temporary loss of memory, remembering nothing of the incident.

When he was demobbed and came back to live in our house, now in Wigan, he was at a loose end. I was suddenly his friend. Whatever I did, wherever I went, Donald wanted to be involved; he wanted to play cricket (and was quite a useful medium-paced bowler), he wanted to go to the pub on a Saturday night, and he even wanted to go to the dance hall. I happened to be involved with my twelve week girl at the time.

'When we go in the dance hall, this girl will be there that I'm going out with. I meet her inside when we've finished cricket and I've had a couple of drinks. She'll want to dance with me all the time. Sometimes she wants to leave early.'

'Can you not forget about her for a couple of weeks until I get sorted out?'

'I'll tell you what, she always has a friend with her while she's waiting for me. I can introduce you. You might like her.'

'Well, OK, but I've had enough of women; they only cause trouble.'

So I found myself on the dance floor, leaving Donald with Doreen, the other girl. The next time I saw them was on the upstairs balcony with their arms around each other. Within nine months, they were married, and Donald finally left our house for good.

# My First Saturday Night Out

'You're not having a key.' These words, spoken by my stepmother, had an ominous ring of finality about them.

Despite having successfully negotiated one Saturday night out for myself, I reluctantly realised I was close to my limit, but risked her backtracking on this permission by persisting with my plea for a key.

'It's only for one night, and I promise I won't lose it. If I don't have a key how am I going to get into the house?'

'Listen, if you want to go gallivanting off to Blackpool you'd better get home at a decent time. We're not waiting up half the night for you.'

I knew it was useless, so took what would have been my grandmother's advice: a bird in the hand is worth two in the bush. The Saturday night event, organised by my work colleagues, was the main objective. I had already negotiated being on that charabanc taking us to the Winter Gardens; not wanting to squander this limited success, with regard to the problem of returning home in the early hours of Sunday morning, I stayed silent. It would have been unwise to suggest leaving the door unlocked, even though this was normal procedure when I set off for my early morning paper round. In fact, one more word on the subject would be the last straw.

I could hardly wait for the day to arrive. It wasn't a day trip; it was generally agreed that a full day out would be too expensive, so our booking was for an evening trip direct to the Winter Gardens.

The charabanc, filled with happy, carefree colleagues from the engineering works, set off on its journey. I felt relaxed. I knew every man on the coach. About three-quarters of them had brought their wives or girlfriends. The conversation was light-hearted and jocular, though what was immediately noticeable, was the absence of bad language from the same men whose working conversation would be filled with obscenities. Their usual coarseness and crudity was replaced by humorous innuendo. The atmosphere on that coach on my first ever Saturday night out was warm and pleasant.

The Winter Gardens was a wonderful sight. The ballroom was spacious, with wide, plush, carpeted stairways leading off through ornate pillared archways to the upstairs balcony or the downstairs drinking areas. There were rooms adjacent to the ballroom available for those who said, 'Let's sit down and have a rest. I'm not as fit as I used to be.' Moments after our party entered the Winter Gardens, it disappeared, dispersed in the crowd. From my breathing space on the balcony, I looked down amazed, wondering how people could move, let alone dance.

If anybody were to ask me how I spent my first Saturday night out, my answer would be simple: from a dance hall balcony, I watched a crowd of people moving slowly to the rhythm of a band. Then I bravely went to buy my first ever drink at a bar, an orange juice, and took it back upstairs. My first Saturday night out was wonderful.

I thought everything was perfect and nothing could spoil this night. But somebody tried. It happened when I decided to go back downstairs for my second drink of orange. The bar area was nearly empty, though luckily for me, there were several people enjoying a quiet drink. I approached the bar, now feeling more confident, and waited patiently for someone to come and serve me. I felt good. Suddenly, I was whisked round, my tie and collar were grabbed, and I was struggling to breathe.

'Who said you could come in here? You're just a puny kid. This is a place for men.' This drunken youth, slurring out these words, was nearly strangling me. My futile struggles seemed to encourage him.

'I don't like your face and I'm going to punch it.'

Then, just as suddenly as it started, it stopped. The stranglehold disappeared. The drunken bully was forcibly pinned to the bar by two men, while a third man was repeating the bully's threat.

'I don't like *your* face and I'm going to punch it.'

The bully wasn't punched, but was immediately frogmarched away and out of the Winter Gardens.

'How do you feel, lad?' was the general enquiry.

'I don't know. I'm not sure what happened. Why did he do that? I've never seen him before.' I was in slight shock and was starting to ramble.

'People do daft things when they're drunk. But never mind, you'll never see him again,' said one of the men who'd saved me. 'You'll feel better when you've had a drink. What are you drinking, lad? Do you want a pint, or a whisky?'

'Can I have a glass of orange juice?'

'You certainly can, and you deserve it.'

The rest of the night was incident-free, but, remaining very wary of meeting up with that drunken bully, I waited near the main exit for the friendly, familiar faces of my work colleagues. In their company I felt safe walking the short distance to the coach.

I hadn't worked out a solution to the key problem, but it must have been evolving somewhere in my subconscious, because by the start of the return journey, I was fully aware of what needed to be done. I asked the coach driver to drop me off in Preston, about five miles from home, using the pretence that I was staying the rest of the night at a relative's. The plan was to walk the five miles back to Leyland, in time to deliver the Sunday papers.

I alighted from the coach at about one o'clock with the friendly farewells and the resigned reality of 'see you at work on Monday morning' ringing in my ears. The way home was easy to navigate, first down a long, steep hill where, at some point, the last houses were left behind, then, at the bottom of the hill, walk about two hundred yards and turn left. This semi-rural road would now take me to the paper shop.

I hadn't reached halfway down the hill when I began to feel disturbed. The drunken bully was still very fresh in my memory, and now there would be no one to save me. The semi-darkness was both ally and enemy; he couldn't see me, but I couldn't see him. I would probably hear him, though, before he heard me, especially if he was drunk. I narrowed my safety options down to either hiding in the hedgerow or running at my fastest speed. Luckily, things went my way. It was a warm night in late spring, with no harsh rain or wind, and thankfully, I didn't see a solitary person during the entire five miles.

My subconscious, however, had plunged me into a strange and frightening situation. I faced five miles walking alone in semi-darkness. The moonlight cast eerie and unrecognisable shapes; sometimes the moon hid behind clouds and there was nothing but darkness. I was also continually subjected to scary scuttling noises in the hedgerows. The drunken bully took second place. Instead of walking close to the hedge, which would offer a quick escape route, I found myself walking down the middle of the open road. I walked through this mysterious darkness into a magnificent morning chorus and the light of a beautiful sunrise. I could now see, clearly, the road that lay ahead.

Eventually, I left the hedgerows behind and made my way through the deserted but now familiar streets to the paper shop.

The Sunday morning paper bag was always the heaviest of the week, and that morning, after my first Saturday night out and my frightening five-mile walk, was no exception. In fact, it felt twice as heavy as normal. Having arrived early, I had first choice of delivery rounds; I chose the shortest, the only disadvantage being the long walking distance from the shop to the starting point of the delivery. This walk was painful. I was feeling weak with hunger, and tired and weary from the Saturday night's activities. Close to the delivery point, I had to pass over the railway bridge. The temptation was too much. Familiar with the embankment, having sometimes sat there thinking about happier times, I couldn't resist. Clambering through the hedgerow, bordering the embankment, I manoeuvred myself into a secluded position and promptly fell asleep. I woke up in mid-afternoon, and never stopped running until the last paper was delivered.

Suffice to say, the following Sunday, I was sacked, no questions asked, no reasons requested. This despite having completed more than one hundred Sunday deliveries without a hint of unreliability. I had never realised that my first Saturday night out could cause such mental, physical and financial disruption. But it was still a wonderful night.

# Growing Independence

'What are the tea chests for?' Half a dozen had suddenly appeared in the front room.

'We'll be moving house soon,' said my stepmother.

'Oh, no, not again. Where are we going this time?'

'We're going back to Wigan.'

'Wigan? Why are we going there?'

'Because your dad wants to and I want to. I can't stand this place.'

'But what about work? I'm not changing my job.'

'You can get to work on the train. I've had to travel to Wigan for the past six years and I've had enough.' My stepmother had paid regular visits to her relatives during this time.

'But it's so far away.'

'Listen, if you want to moan, moan at your dad. We're moving to Wigan and that's it.'

'I'm not moaning, I'm just fed up. This is stupid. I'm not going. I can't stand it. Donald thought you were all stupid – he said it was the best day of his life when he was called up. I'm going to – '

'Shut up. Shut your bloody noise. Just get out of my sight. Will you never grow up?'

When my dad was alone in the sitting room, I tried again.

'When are we moving?'

'Soon.'

'I don't want to go.'

'You've no choice.'

'But what about my life? My weight training and cricket and table tennis? It'll all disappear.'

'You're only a young lad. You'll soon settle down.'

'But I'm settled down here.'

'Look, we're moving and that's it.'

'But why? Just tell me why.'

'Because I'm after another job. You'll be catching the train. In fact, I'll be catching the train until I get another job.'

I mentally established that I wouldn't be sitting in the same compartment as my dad.

'And listen to me,' he continued. 'Don't speak to your mother like you did earlier. She's doing her best. This could be a real home if you tried.'

I was upset enough to feel brave.

'What do you mean, if I tried? I'm just a skivvy. Donald was glad when he left. He said it was the best day of his life, and he said this was a stupid house. You've not helped me. All you do is sit in that armchair reading the paper or falling asleep, or else you disappear off to your club. You don't know what I've to put up with. I've got a list of jobs a mile long, and all you say is that this could be a real home if I tried. I'll never be happy here and I'm not moving.'

'Just go. Just leave me in peace. We're moving, and that's it.' Surprisingly, he didn't react more to my emotional outburst.

I now attended my evening pleasures with diminishing enthusiasm and a sense of increasing loneliness. My parents had discussed, planned and decided to put into operation this next house move. Their objective, reached twelve months after the actual move, was to be stewards of one of the many social clubs in Wigan. The reason for the early move was that Keith would be starting secondary school, and it went without saying that it was essential for him to start and finish in the one school. In the twelve months waiting for the stewardship, my dad continued at Leyland Motors, getting up at half past five, catching a local bus to town, then a train, finally walking to the works and clocking in by 7:30. For his return journey, he left work at five o'clock and arrived home at about 6:30. If I were to complete my apprenticeship, that journey would be mine for the next two and a half years. Again, it went without saying that my apprenticeship would be completed; according to my dad: 'You must be skilled. You're no good in life if you haven't served an apprenticeship.'

Ironically, this move speeded up my independence. If we had continued living in Leyland, who knows how long the status quo would have lasted. At that time, I hadn't realised that, though I had always felt young, my days at the youth club would have been over, since it catered for fifteen to eighteen-year-olds. Also, at seven and a half stone and five feet tall, though the struggle for permanent second eleven cricket would still have continued, with these physical handicaps, I would have remained languishing as first reserve. Consequently, my hopes might slowly have receded and I probably would have lost heart for the game. Finally, my weight training for definition could easily have turned into training for bulk, and this, even for an eighteen-year-old going on twelve, would still have been stupid.

This new move was in more ways than one a completely fresh start. I was no longer required to look after Keith. He more or less immediately began spending time with my stepmother's relatives, which freed me from babysitting duties. I was just told of the new arrangements. 'From now on, you can keep your wages and pay three pounds a week for food and board. You pay your own bus and train fare to work. You buy all your own clothes. You can go out any time you want, as long as you catch the last bus home.'

All this was difficult to follow, but eventually, I began to follow the gist. I was to become a lodger, paying three pounds a week for food and sleeping accommodation. The remainder of my wages was mine to spend how, where and when I liked. I could also stay out seven nights a week until the last bus from town, which left at 10:55 and got me to my lodgings at 11:10. Far from feeling rejected by the abruptness of these changes, I felt ecstatic. This new independence was much stronger after my immediate and successful request to add to these changes. It was agreed that, as a lodger, my assistance was no longer required in any of the household chores, except to wash up my own pots. I didn't need to clean out the grate or make the fire (though it was annoying, after all my years chopping wood, to see firelighters suddenly appear in the house), or do any shopping except voluntarily for odd necessities from the corner shop.

The ecstasy quickly vanished when I started to think. I knew nobody in this town, and would have to go alone to strange new places. And it was all right catching the last bus home, but from where? The new lightness of my household chores seemed to coincide with a new heaviness in my heart, which was worse than all the household chores put together. It had always been there, surfacing occasionally, but my previous lifestyle had kept it at bay.

In fact, from the time when I was told to stand at the dining table to eat, until the time we returned to the Wigan area, I had been continually rejected and isolated, with any complaints, for whatever reason, being a waste of time. Consequently, prolonged arguments were few. Any protests had always been cut short, sometimes at the first word, and dismissed out of hand. There were many times when my rebellion against that life had simply taken the form of silence; for days and days, I was like a zombie, doing all my jobs without speaking a word to my parents. This also had irritated them.

'When I shout for you to come here, it's good manners to answer.' Silence.

'Do you hear what I'm saying?' Silence.

'Why don't you answer me?'

I just stared and remained silent. I didn't speak and they couldn't make me speak. These silent confrontations always ended in the same way.

'Oh, get out of my sight!'

I left the room feeling I'd achieved a minor triumph, glad they couldn't handle the situation.

Such responses had helped me to cope, though weight-training, table tennis and cricket, filling all my spare time, had been my main consolation and escape.

But now, for much of the time, this loneliness, with nothing to combat it, completely filled my heart. For the next two and a half years, it dominated. I was living a lonely life in lodgings. The move back to Wigan had become a crucial time in my teenage years. I was eighteen, but still very much an adolescent, my emotional growth stunted by a lack of love and guidance.

It was certainly no state of languishing, of feeling sorry for myself, though. I knew something had to be done; as my grandma would say, simply, 'Where there's a will there's a way.' I turned to cricket, but now strictly within the lower limits. By scanning the local evening and weekly papers, I worked out the nearest team to my house; that is, the nearest team playing cricket in one of the lower leagues. I then went to watch them play and spoke to the captain, who suggested I keep turning up on the off-chance. The team was such that I was in it the following week, playing in normal clothes. Within a month, I had bought cricket whites and a pair of boots. It wasn't a high standard, but those two summers were the best I ever had playing cricket. What was enjoyable, as much as the bowling, slip fielding and batting, was the friendly banter and general camaraderie – in the dressing room, out on the field, in the tea room, and playing away, when, if bus routes were difficult, the travelling was by car.

Quite soon after joining my new team, I was sitting in my first pub since the days of visiting my other grandad's, but this time having my first alcoholic drink, a pint of bitter, price one shilling and two pence. So the summer time Saturdays took on a familiar and enjoyable pattern of cricket and pub. Later on, at the invitation of a couple of the lads in the cricket team, I found myself going dancing.

At first, just the atmosphere in the dance hall was enough, so I didn't mind paying two and six, and never having a dance. The band and resident singers were terrific, and the girls, looking distantly attractive in their Saturday best, made the dance hall a warm and comfortable place to be. Eventually, I found enough courage to ask a girl for a dance. This courage then strengthened, and I asked a girl for a date. These dates were always the same. I would meet a girl on Sunday afternoon, walk with her in the park and take her, me paying, to one of the numerous picture places in town. That would be it. It's strange, but I never asked a girl for a second date, just saying, 'Cheerio,' like an American, and, 'See you in the dance hall.'

It was months down the line of Sunday dates before I dared to kiss a girl. After that, I kissed them on every date and thought I was like a great screen lover, like Rudolf Valentino.

Then, when I was about twenty, I met a girl who seemed different from the others and made much more of an impression on me. We went to the pictures more than once. In fact, we went out together for nearly three months. She was a nice looking girl, a smaller version of Kim Novak, an attractive film star. When we were out walking on Sunday afternoons, it was like the "American girl" together in the park, more often than not with her arm wrapped around me. Sometimes I felt a bit scared, especially when I was drawn into one of her clinches. I thought

I must be in love. However, when she started to plan a holiday at Butlin's, I packed her in.

Now that I was a lodger and had progressed from Friday night youth club to Saturday dance, a vital and comforting influence from my schooldays was strengthened. This was my liking for the ever-changing popular songs and singers. My initial interest had been entirely limited to observing the boys mimicking their favourites, usually, according to the girls, poor imitations. I also listened to their arguments as to who was the best singer; this was normally a contest between Johnny Ray and Frankie Laine, but Frank Sinatra would sometimes enter the equation. Then came *Bill Haley and his Comets*. Their music seemed to cause unfriendly and aggressive behaviour, which frightened me. I preferred the sounds of *Secret Love*, *Answer Me*, *The Man from Laramie*, *Rose Marie*, *Softly, Softly* and similar ballads. I heard these songs only very occasionally before I started going to the youth club, but throughout my regular two-hour table tennis sessions, starting on that first evening with *Sixteen Tons*, the background music was always the past, the recent past and the latest most popular singers and songs.

Now, in the dance hall, instead of being just background music, it took on a greater importance. I was dancing to these songs performed by a live band and resident singers. Also, on any summer Saturday afternoon when not playing cricket, and on many winter Saturdays, I spent time in the local record shop. Since I had become quite friendly with the girl behind the counter, she turned a blind eye to the length of time I stayed in the booths, listening to all the latest records and to those others that I particularly liked. I was introduced to new songs like *All Shook Up, Young Love, Diana, Singing the Blues, Butterfly*, to add to the ones I liked from the "oldies" such as *Just Walking in the Rain, A Woman in Love, No Other Love, The Finger of Suspicion* and so on. Inevitably, I eventually bought a record player; it could hold eight records when fully loaded. I bought my two favourites, Pat Boone's *April Love* and *Love Letters in the Sand.* Gradually, I had enough records to fill my record player, giving me about twenty-five minutes' listening time. The last record I bought while I was living in Wigan would be Paul Anka's *Lonely Boy*.

Despite many hours listening to and enjoying these records, I could never remember all of the words; I seemed to stop somewhere between the second and fourth line, just happily repeating the same few lines of whatever song I felt like singing. The shortened lyrics were probably a defence against my double handicap: first, I could never, even remotely, imitate the singer's voice, and second, I could never sing in tune. But at work, this didn't matter – nobody could hear me. The deafening noise of the belt-driven machines drowned out my two and four line versions of *All Shook Up, Teddy Bear, Heartbreak Hotel* and *Hound Dog*, *Diana*, *Lonely Boy*, *It's Only Make Believe* and many more, all suitable for my rendition, and all lost in the bedlam.

In the quieter phases of my life, away from work, I changed my tune; if no one was in hearing distance, I could confidently become Tab Hunter singing *Young Love*, Tex Ritter singing *The Wayward Wind*, Elvis singing *Love Me Tender*, Andy Williams singing *Lonely Street*, and many more.

The move to Wigan had forced me to stop weight training and table tennis. I continued to play cricket, but had now been introduced to alcohol, dancing and girls, and those very important songs. I even tried my hand at writing a hit song, or at least the lyrics of one:

All you cats hear my call,
Come along with me
To the County Hall, Where the floor is square
But we've got the beat.
Come on everybody,
It sure is sweet.
At the ball
In the County Hall.

Fortunately, I can't remember any more.

Thanks to the Musical Express, I paid about two pounds to have music put to my lyrics and I was ready for the big time. I sent the song to Jack Jackson, who had been very popular in the thirties and forties during the big band era and was now a disc jockey with his own Saturday morning radio show. Although I got a brief handwritten reply, my song was rejected. The blow was softened by the suggestion that it could possibly be a B-side, but with plenty of these available, I should keep trying for a "hit".

I didn't bother writing any more lyrics, probably because my other interests began to distract me, one in particular.

# When Is a Girl Not a Girl?

The Teddy Boy cult was sweeping the country, and I had the opportunity to join the local group. Two of my weekend friends tried their best to persuade me, but I resisted. The thought of wearing a long draped jacket, drainpipe trousers and thick crepe-soled shoes made me scared, as did the thought of being part of the "bully boy" groups, who roamed the Saturday night streets looking for trouble. I was often forced into making a detour rather than risk a head-on clash. One of my fellow apprentices was a stalwart member of a Saturday night bully gang, but strangely, he was always pleasant and friendly at work. One day, I asked him point-blank why he spent his Saturday nights looking for trouble. His answer: 'I need an outlet from this boredom. A good punch-up at the weekend makes me feel better.'

I agreed with him with regard to boredom, but didn't rock the boat. I didn't tell him I had found better things to do than fighting, but occasionally, looked at him working and wondered if all the gang members were living just to spend Saturday night looking for trouble. Thankfully, I never had the urge to join in any punch-ups, whatever the day.

So, my chosen framework helped me to feel safe and secure, but within this comfortable existence, certain situations occurred that affected me and raised a few testing questions. For instance, take the warning words of my grandma:

'Alan, you can't rely on losing a bad penny – it keeps turning up.'

This particular bad penny was the annual works holiday fortnight. I had always found holidays difficult to face, ending up in the same isolated, lonely, rejected state.

My parents had never done anything to help me.

'Right, you've got plenty of time to get your jobs done.'

'But I'm on holiday.'

'Yes, but you don't play out till you've done all your jobs.'

'What about you? What are you doing?'

'Never mind me, you cheeky imp.'

'Well, what about Keith? He does nothing, and he laughs at me. If he laughs at me again I'm going to thump him.'

'Listen, if you touch Keith I'll thrash the living daylights out of you. Just get out and chop that bloody firewood and then take this bloody list to Wardle's.'

My stepmother and Keith regularly disappeared early in the morning to visit her Wigan relatives, leaving me with a list of jobs. Quite often, Keith stayed with those relatives for parts of the school holidays. On these days, I could at least smoke in peace and eat toast and butter.

I tried to compensate whenever possible. One school holiday, I lived with my dog, another I spent every day in the countryside, having made myself a vow to become the owner of the largest birds' egg collection in the world. Mostly I was a secondary member of the neighbourhood children's group activities.

So once again, when I was nineteen, the bad penny turned up. This time I had worked out the perfect solution, even though it went against the grain of my grandad's wise words – 'Never volunteer.'

I filled in a form in the local paper offering my labouring services for a fortnight at one of the many cotton mills around the county. This was the perfect solution; not only would this job help me through the holiday, but I would also be paid for it. I could see the bad penny turning into gold.

This mill was about twenty miles away, in either Oldham or Rochdale. Each morning, coaches transported mill workers from outlying towns to their place of work. When I caught my coach on that first Monday morning, I stared in disbelief: it was filled with women. Apart from the driver, I was the only male. Instantly, there was a volley of lively comments.

'Oh, look what we've got here!'

'Oo, love, come and sit next to me!'

'Don't sit next to her, love. Come and sit on my knee!'

This was only six o'clock in the morning. What would happen as the day progressed? Luckily, there was a single seat to the left of the driver, which stopped me from retreating to the safety of the pavement.

It was the same inside the mill. Wherever I looked, the workers were women. The noise of the machines was deafening, so that sometimes I understood the machine workers only by their sign language. I couldn't ignore them, because it was part of my job to fulfil their demands and to fetch, carry and clean. It was hard to distinguish between the real requests and the "cry wolf" signs, the suggestive smiles, the alluring poses and the beckoning enticements. The secret was not to be cornered; luckily, the massive shop floor area provided me with enough space to manage this.

The coach was different. The seat by the driver was essential, so every morning and evening, I scurried to it. However, early in the first week, I rushed to the coach after work and found, to my horror, the seat was occupied.

'Can I have my seat, please?' I asked nervously.

'Oh, no, love. You'll have to go and sit next to that girl down there,' she said, pointing.

I stared at her, this mill-girl, as they liked to be called. I had never been so close to one. Her eyes were laughing at me. Then I followed the direction of her pointing finger, knowing full-well what it would reveal.

The coach was suddenly strangely silent. I felt like crawling along that centre aisle in search of an empty seat. I did manage to retain some sanity, though, enough to enable me to creep, with lowered face, past all the laughing eyes.

It must have been a deliberate decision of theirs to ensure the empty seat was the furthest distance from the front. I sank into the seat, and was immediately sandwiched between two mill-girls of the seductive type. They both put their arms around me and the entire coach burst into laughter.

'Come on, love, give me a cuddle.'

'Never mind her, love, snuggle up to me. Come on, it's a long drive home. We can have some fun.'

Both girls started squeezing and stroking me tantalisingly.

'Feel these muscles! Ooh, give me a big kiss.'

Suddenly, one of them leaned over and put her arms around me; I found my face sinking into her body.

'Come here, love.' The other one took over and with the coach cheering, pulled me away from her rival's clutches and immediately gave me a powerful kiss. I felt it was an achievement to keep them at bay, but I think they were just playing a game with me – putting me through the mill.

Dinner times were also dangerous. Weather permitting, the usual practice was to eat your lunch sitting on the grassy areas around the factory.

'Come and sit here, love, so we can talk. You can't hear yourself think with them machines.'

'What's your name, love?'

'Alan.'

'Ooh, that's a nice name. You look like Alan Ladd.'

'I think our Alan looks nicer than him.'

'What a lovely day. Let's lie down in this warm sun.'

'Come on, Alan love, rest your head near mine.'

'Come on, love, you look sad. I'll make you happy.'

'Sit closer, Alan. I promise I won't torment you.'

If they had wanted to turn serious, I would have been in real trouble. However, at the time, those two weeks gave this very young nineteen-year-old, striving for whatever, an incredibly enlightening insight into the wiles and wooings of women.

Despite feeling my grandad would frown and look at me disapprovingly ('I told you never to volunteer, lad'), I was still glad to have subjected myself to the mill girls' ordeal, especially now, with my pockets full of gold.

A few short weeks later, a similar predicament arose from a visit to the doctor. The visit was voluntary, but the doctor took over with such effect that within three days, I was sitting up, eating my dinner, in a hospital bed. Even though all this was for the best, I suppose my grandad, seeing me there, would have considered it another reason for never volunteering.

The prediction was that I would be home within five days, but my stay in hospital was extended to fourteen days, with a further fourteen days of daily attendance. The concern didn't arise from complications, but from the danger of infection. There was no option but to follow instructions, which meant that for about twenty-one days, twice a day, I found myself sitting completely naked in a bath of tepid water mixed with infection-reducing medication, under the watchful eyes of either Nurse

Barton or Nurse Heaton. I will never forget their names. Despite their total commitment, care and kindness, the situation was, of course, difficult for a nineteen-year-old young man.

'Come on, Alan, it's time for your morning bath.'

'Can I not leave it till afternoon?'

'Now, Alan, you know you have to have another one in the afternoon. Come on now, the bath's ready. You go and get in. I'll be there in a minute.'

'OK, nurse,' I said resignedly, and hurried to get undressed and in the bath before she came back.

Nurse Heaton was the most frightening; she reminded me of the mill girls.

'Ooh, Alan, you look different without any clothes on. I thought you'd be all skin and bone. Look at your muscles. Your body feels nice and firm and strong.' All the time sponging me down.

In those early, scary bathing days, I found it difficult to speak to her, but eventually managed to find some courage; it was time to get my own back.

'I've been thinking about you, nurse.'

'Ooh, tell me.'

'Well, I've been thinking I'll bet you look different without any clothes on. I wish I was a nurse and you were sitting here in this bath and I was sponging you all over. I've been wondering what your body feels like.'

If I'd been expecting her to be embarrassed, I was disappointed.

'Ooh, Alan, if I was ill, I'd like you to be my nurse. I wouldn't be shy like you.' My courage instantly disappeared.

'Can I get out now and put my clothes on?' I was still frightened of Nurse Heaton.

Nurse Barton seemed different. She tried to make me feel relaxed.

'Well, Alan, how do you spend your time?'

'What do you mean?'

'Well, what do you do for a living? What do you do when you're not working?'

'I'm learning a trade in an engineering works, and I play cricket every Saturday.'

'Do you go dancing?'

'I usually go to the Empress Hall after cricket.'

'Oh, I go there sometimes.'

I was being cornered again.

'Can I get out now? Can I go back to bed?'

'Yes, but listen, I'll look for you so we can have a dance. Do you know how to smooch?'

Nurse Barton had suddenly become Nurse Heaton. The two of them were like all the mill girls rolled into one.

In between these bathing treatments, I would help out in the ward, busying myself taking the drinks round to the patients, helping with the laundry, tidying the nurses' staffroom and helping at lunch – with a slap-up meal for myself.

The ward sister was male. For some reason, he singled me out for special favours. Every day, during my last week, he hid a bottle of Guinness in my bedside cabinet, warning me not to tell anyone. I didn't; I just enjoyed the Guinness.

Before these experiences, I didn't have an opinion about girls, except that they were nice, and I liked to be in their company. But it seemed they could be even more dangerous and frightening than the bully boys. This didn't prevent me from dancing with girls and enjoying their company; I just had to be more careful. Never again would I be trapped by a smiling temptress. I had been taken into unfamiliar territory and returned feeling less safe and secure.

It may have been coincidence, but it was about this time that my visits to the pub became more frequent.

# A Reprobate Saved

I began the evening in the pub, sometimes not leaving until closing time.

Playing darts and dominoes was enjoyable, but not without a drink. Even before a Sunday afternoon date, I visited the pub before meeting the girl. Like smoking, when the one cigarette each day soon doubled, then trebled, my drinking habit started with one visit to one pub for one drink, but soon multiplied to become seven nights and weekend afternoons. It got worse, in that a dinner time pub visit in the working day became a necessity. Unaware of any harm this could be doing to me, I just liked to drink; drinking helped me to feel good. I was never argumentative, just friendly and cheerful, not realising that I wasn't happy without the aid of a drink. Nobody had shown any disapproval, so any dangers went unnoticed. Nevertheless, I needed help. This came from an unexpected source.

When an apprentice reached the age of eighteen, he could be called upon to work a night shift. The system was to work two weeks on day shift, then two weeks on night shift, being paid extra for nights. At first, I didn't want to work nights, but now, nearly twenty years old and needing drinking money, when night shift opportunities arose, I took them. One night, during the "dinner" break, I sat with a man of about twenty-five who never swore, never told crude jokes and never discussed intimate details of past or present girlfriends. Normally, this was what dinner times served up, but this man was different. He seemed happy to listen to my ramblings about cricket, records, singers and the Saturday night dance, but the turning point came when he asked me a question.

'What would you prefer, to die, whenever that may be, in the distant future, or to live forever in a much better world?'

Then he said, 'I could prove to you how you could live forever in this better world.' I became interested, and the midnight conversations continued.

This man, Colin, lived in a similar direction to my lodgings; there was a distance between us of about five miles. For the next three or four months, I spent two nights each week attending Bible Study sessions, becoming so engrossed that I also went to Sunday meetings. In fact, my Sunday timetable included knocking on people's doors to discuss the wickedness in the world and suggest a way of escape, attending the Sunday meeting and spending two hours in the evening at Bible Study.

Colin had an old motor car, and on the occasions that the class went over time and I missed the bus, he drove me home. On one November night, there was an extremely dense fog. Two or three hundred yards into the journey, with the fog throwing back the beam of the headlight, on a narrow, unpaved and unlit road, there was a thud.

'Oh, no, I've hit somebody!'

Colin scrambled out of the car to investigate, shouting for me to get out as well.

A dark shape lay on the ground by the side of the road. It appeared to be an elderly man. He wasn't moving.

'Alan, you stay here while I drive to a phone box. Don't touch him, but keep talking to him. Tell him I've gone to phone for an ambulance. I'll be as quick as I can, OK?'

'Right, Colin, but hurry up!' I spoke for the first time. Now, left in the blackness, I could think of nothing to do except repeatedly tell the moaning shape that someone had gone for an ambulance, and that it wouldn't be long. The man's groans penetrated the darkness and silent mist. I was afraid. It was a long fifteen minutes before Colin's welcome return.

'Right, the ambulance is on its way. How is he?'

'I don't know. He's still moaning. I think he's dying.' I couldn't stop shaking.

Colin knelt down next to the shape on the floor, patting the man gently and whispering softly until finally the ambulance arrived and took him to hospital. We went back to Colin's house.

'I'll make a pot of tea, you just sit near the fire.' Colin was keeping busy. My whole body was shaking with cold and trembling with fright, brought on by delayed shock.

'I thought he was going to die.' It was me that was moaning now.

'Thank God, it wasn't that bad. The ambulance man said it was broken bones. He thinks he'll be all right. I never saw him.'

'It wasn't your fault, Colin.'

'I hope not. How are you now? Sorry, I had to leave you there, but someone had to stay with him. Did nobody else stop?'

'Nobody came past. Eee, Colin, I didn't think you'd come back.'

'You did well staying with him, Alan, especially in that pitch black. I don't know what I would have done if I'd been left on my own.'

Colin spent some time making tea and calming both of us down.

Eventually, he drove me home at about one in the morning. My parents were in the living room. I went in and closed the door, having decided to tell them about the accident. Suddenly I was grabbed, lifted bodily and pinned forcibly against the door. People say that when you are close to sudden death your whole life flashes by in a matter of moments. In that moment of bodily lift-off, I saw only two pairs of eyes. My stepmother's, glinting in satisfaction as she witnessed the start of what she thought would be something worth waiting for. My dad's warning of his pent-up fury, soon to be released on me. Before this force could be unleashed, I shouted out the words, 'I've killed somebody!' This stopped him in his tracks. My feet touched the ground again and I instantly ran to the safety of my bedroom. My dad followed me upstairs, and after listening to my explanation and seeing how shook up I was, he actually apologised. We returned to the living room and I gave them a full account of the night's events.

This incident was a major turning point. Shortly afterwards, having realised that I had grown weary of this life, I decided to leave, but not immediately. It would have been foolish to throw away all that time, effort and accomplishment by going, when I would soon be twenty-one and then my apprenticeship would be completed. Besides, I needed to work out a plan. A little caution now could prevent a lot of danger later. This prudence was most important because I would never have been able to return to this life again. The decision to complete my apprenticeship gave me enough time to get organised, to think where the best course would lie. The Bible Classes were stopped. I felt a genuine hesitancy over this decision; in fact, this was my hardest moment. I had to sever this connection or become more deeply involved in this way of life. If I continued Bible Studies, I would have been distracted from my fundamental determination, which was not only to leave my lodgings but also to quit the area completely.

The termination of the Bible Studies freed me from any form of commitment that might persuade me to stay. So, with nothing to hold me back, I could start to make definite plans. During the interim, while waiting to disappear, I returned to my previous lifestyle, with one welcome exception. Now no longer needing to drink every spare minute of the day, I could even go to the Saturday night dance without first visiting the pub. I did usually have a pint or two, but now my drinking was definitely social rather than a matter of necessity.

# Two Good Moves

Just two or three weeks after the bodily lift-off, we moved house again, but this time I found it a much more favourable move. My dad became the steward of a social club in a large stone Victorian building in the entertainment area of Wigan town centre, family accommodation being provided on the second floor. Access, day or night, was first through the heavy wooden front door; then there was a wide marble staircase, with a well-worn but deeply polished dark wooden bannister, and a lift. I always took the lift. It was an iron-grilled cage; when in operation, I could observe the bustling activity on the ground floor and the first floor, until they faded out of sight. There were several thriving businesses on these two floors, mainly solicitors, accountants and typing agencies. Their waiting rooms, visible through smoked glass in dark partitions, always seemed full of shadowy people. The lift was similar to those I had seen in the pictures, especially the gangster films. In the daytime, when using this lift, I became a film star, my affections and amateur acting ability being shared equally between the hoodlum and the detective. At night, in the empty silence, I was the detective, searching out the hoodlums crouched in dark corners; when caught, the iron-grilled cage would be their prison. Sometimes, though, as I opened the cage doors, reality returned and I would find myself scurrying through the gloom to the safety of the flat.

There were two reasons why this move was favourable for me. First, it reduced the travelling time to and from work, as there was no bus to catch, morning or evening. The train station was just a five minute walk from my new lodgings; in fact, the bus stop where I had got off every morning was right opposite my new lodging house, so the walking time didn't change. The second advantage was more important, in that I didn't need to catch the last bus home. Wherever I decided to go in the evenings or at weekends, the dance hall, picture place or snooker hall, it was never more than a ten minute walk from my new lodgings; in fact, fifty yards to the right was my Saturday afternoon record shop; fifty yards to the left was the Court Hall, both a cinema and a dance hall. Directly across the street from my lodgings was the County picture place. The Court and the County, along with the Ritz, were the top cinemas, vying to be the first to show the latest film. The other four picture places in town seemed to show these new releases six months later.

In the basement area beneath the picture place directly opposite was a large snooker hall. I had taken up snooker as a winter activity to replace cricket. Snooker being a sport you can enjoy playing alone, it was a welcome pastime on those cold and rainy Saturday afternoons. The cost was sixpence for twenty minutes' playing time, so all I needed was a pocketful of sixpences. What could be better? My snooker, of course. Nevertheless, it was great fun.

So, for the first time I could see and appreciate the benefits of my parents moving house. The only drawback was the front door key. It wasn't as enormous as an old gaoler's key but it was certainly large, heavy and awkward; I carried it uncomfortably in the inside pocket of my suit.

Because of this key, on one of my Sunday dates, I nearly found myself in a spot of trouble, or at least having some explaining to do.

'Hello, Jean.'

'Hello. I didn't think you'd remember my name.'

'Have you remembered mine, then?'

'No, I haven't, sorry.'

'Well, it's Alan. Listen, can you just put this key in your handbag? It's weighing me down.'

'What are you carrying that around for?'

'It's the key to a door. Just put it in your handbag.'

'All right, but why are you carrying it about with you?'

This was my third or fourth date since moving to the town centre. I had quickly realised that girls seemed impressed by someone living in a flat in the centre of town. 'It's the key to my flat.'

'It must be a big flat.'

'It is. It's in one of them massive Victorian buildings in town.'

'You've got a flat in the town centre? Really? Can I see it?'

'OK, then. It's only a couple of minutes away.' That was a mistake.

'Here we are. Let's have the key.' I pushed the heavy door open. 'Do you want to go up the stairs or use the lift?'

'Oh, let's go in the lift.'

All I had wanted was for the girl to carry my cumbersome key. I was hoping my parents were at work in the club. Luckily, the flat was empty. The interior doors, as usual, were closed. I took a chance that the kitchen would be tidy and free from clues that it wasn't just my flat.

'We're not staying in. I'll just have this drink of water, then we'll go out.'

'Ooh, what a nice kitchen. Can we not have a cup of tea? I'll make it.'

'No, let's not bother. Do you want to go for a walk or not?'

'Yes, all right then.'

'Right, let's get going. You've seen where I live, right in the middle of town.'

'Oh, yes. It's lovely.'

Relieved, I closed and locked the heavy front door.

Jean took back the key. She came closer to me and linked my arm.

'Alan, I'll never forget your name,' she smiled. 'Eee, I'd like a flat in the town centre.'

After our walk that afternoon, I made sure that she didn't carry my key again.

The move into Wigan town centre didn't influence me in any way to remain in the area. The intention was still the same: I wanted to get away. I would be in one of the last batches to be called up for National Service; to be exempt, would have meant staying on at Leyland Motors and working towards the Higher National Certificate. I didn't want to be exempted, so to avoid any possible complication, I cut out the waiting for call up and applied to join the Royal Air Force as a regular serviceman.

My heart was set on leaving, and I was just waiting for the moment. It was all going to happen when I reached twenty-one. This was usually acknowledged as a special occasion – 'Today you're a man…the key of the door at last…let's drink to your health!'

On my twenty-first birthday, there was no celebration. In fact, it would have been easy to have gone the whole day without seeing my parents, but I decided to go to the club and make myself visible. My stepmother was either looking busy or disappearing into a back room. My dad was serving. Would he mention my birthday?

'Have this on me, lad.'

'Oh, thanks.' He very occasionally bought me a drink, so I wasn't surprised.

'So you managed it, then.'

'Managed what?' I wasn't sure whether I'd managed it to twenty-one or to the end of my apprenticeship. I should have known.'

'You've got a trade. Now you can get a job anywhere.'

'Yes, but now I've finished, I'm going to pack it in.'

'Pack it in? You can't just throw it all away. You're skilled now, you've got a trade, lad.' He seemed genuinely concerned.

'Do you know how old I am?'

'You're twenty-one.'

I waited for him to congratulate me. He didn't.

'Well, that means I'm a man now. I can do what I want, so I'm leaving. I'm leaving my job and I'm leaving here. I'm going to join the RAF. I've already applied.'

Since the bodily lift-off, which wasn't so long before, my dad had stopped waving his fist and telling me to get upstairs.

'Don't you think that's a bit hasty?'

'No. I've waited five years for this. As soon as I'm accepted, I'm handing in my notice.'

'What if you fail the medical?'

'I won't. There's nothing wrong with me.'

'Well, don't pack your job in until you're sure. The RAF medical is strict; they'll fail you on the slightest thing.'

'OK, I won't.' The medical could be a stumbling block, but I didn't want him to see I was concerned. I finished my drink and went off to play snooker.

There was no mention of the specialness of being twenty-one and its being an important milestone in life. This day was special only in its sadness: my parents just didn't care.

Shortly after my twenty-first birthday, I was called for an interview at an RAF Recruitment Centre. After the preliminary interview, numerous forms had to be completed. The one I clearly remember was the form which asked about illnesses and allergies.

'If you suffer from any of the following, please tick the box.' I left the asthma box empty.

'Do you suffer from any allergies? Please list in the box provided.' I left the box completely empty.

About three weeks later, I received notification that my interview had been successful. Along with this wonderful news was a request to attend another RAF centre for a medical. That day was a blur. The entire medical analysis was out of my hands; I couldn't hide things any more. I was aware of my dad's warning about the strictness of the RAF medical, and was unbelievably tense, feeling sure that one of the half-dozen doctors would discover something that would fail me. All that I remember of that medical day are my height and weight statistics: five feet three and a quarter and eight stone seven. So, from sixteen to twenty-one, I grew six and a quarter inches and put on two stones in weight. From that point onwards, I always measured up my fighting weight to be eight stone seven pounds.

The next two weeks were torture. Then I finally received the letter – I had passed the interview, passed the medical, and was to report to the main RAF Recruitment Station at Cardington in early August for a three-day induction. Then, if it became "all systems go", I would be joining the RAF as a regular raw recruit.

Things were moving fast. There had never been any doubts, never any second thoughts, but there was a strong feeling of the unknown soon to be faced. I had often thought that when the day came to hand in my notice at the engineering works, it would be "hip, hip, hooray!", but it just didn't happen. The situation had a very quietening effect on me and, even though I was glad to be leaving, I remained in this subdued state throughout my entire notice.

Finally, almost four months after my twenty-first birthday, and nearly thirteen years of continual rejection, my second life, physically at least, was left behind forever. This moment is clear. At seven o'clock that morning, I closed the heavy door behind me for the last time. There was no one to wish me luck or even to wave goodbye. My parents were still asleep. Very sad and completely alone, in the short walk to the railway station, I was unable to prevent the tears.

# All Too Late

From eight to eighteen, I rarely visited my grandparents. I was leading a life that was strictly regulated by my parents, and, however difficult it is to believe, I never felt the urge to seriously rebel. Not that my grandparents were forgotten. They often entered my thoughts; I found myself asking for their opinion or help, and thinking of what suitable wise words of advice they would offer me. Over those years, I spent many hours reliving life with them; they were not only influential, but also provided me with a strong feeling of protection, making me feel much safer and more at ease with myself, even if sometimes, they seemed to be casting a disapproving eye over my judgement. In a strange way, they were still the cornerstone of my life.

Now, back in Wigan, I was living only a short distance from them. In fact, after taking the bus to town, I was in familiar walking distance. Now that I had a lot more freedom, I could now visit my grandparents at any time.

However, and this is the awful truth, the euphoria of near-total independence and new-found social interests were paramount, to such an extent that twelve months went by, and I was nineteen before I went to visit them.

I had met one of my Sunday afternoon dates; we found ourselves walking down the arcade, past the grammar school and through the American gates into the park. It hadn't changed. We walked by the *keep off the grass* areas to the swings and roundabouts, then past the familiar bowling greens, putting green and tennis courts. Approaching the exit, we passed the point where the American saved Donald from the bullies, then through the gate, across the field, across the road, now without tramlines, and into our field.

We walked up the unevenly-flagged garden path to the open front door. There had been an eleven-year gap, but it seemed natural to just walk in without knocking. We went along the dark passageway, past the front room parlour, to the familiar living room door. I quietly opened it. Grandma was busy in the kitchen.

'Hello, Grandma. I thought I would come and see you.'

She turned round and stared in disbelief. Still staring, she came right up to me.

'It's Alan! I can't believe it! Let me have a good look at you. My word, you've grown up. Let me tell your grandad. He's in his greenhouse. Oh, Alan, I can't believe it!'

Grandad came into the house.

'Hello, Grandad. I thought I'd come and see you.'

He just stared at me.

'Sit down, Grandad. I'll make us all a cup of tea. Hasn't he grown up? I can't believe it.' She went into the kitchen, leaving Grandad to cope.

He finally spoke his first words. 'I'll give you a tomato after our tea.'

'Thanks, Grandad. I've been wondering about the tomatoes and the chrysanthemums. I've been wondering if you were able to cope without my help. I mean, Grandad, I had to do everything, didn't I? You just seemed to sit in your wicker chair, smoking your pipe.'

He now looked at me with twinkling eyes and a slight shake of the head.

'Eee, thar a rum lad.'

My grandparents didn't seem to have changed. I suppose that, to a little boy, they looked old. Now, they still looked just as old to me as a young man. One noticeable difference that I realised about my grandad was his physical frailty. I had always thought of him as being old but strong.

The friendly interrogation by my grandparents, who were pleased with my physical development, led to me proudly challenging my grandad to a test of strength. This involved standing face to face with hands palm down and fingers locked, the one with the strongest grip and wrists eventually forcing his opponent into submission or the humiliation of lying prostrate on the floor. It was Grandma who warned me.

'Grandad, be careful. You don't want to break your wrists again.'

There are moments when you just know, and for me, this was such a moment. As soon as I took hold of my grandad's hands, I knew I was stronger than him. I could see in his eyes a mixture of excitement and panic. Making up my mind instantly, I pretended to put up some genuine resistance, and gradually gave in to him. As he forced me down, I was glad to see the gleam of triumph in his eyes.

In the aftermath of the initial excitement, I did manage to introduce my Sunday date. Whilst Grandma was quizzing her, with Grandad chuckling to himself and filling his pipe from his familiar leather pouch, I had a good look around the room.

It was just as I remembered, with the large, shiny black dresser and wide mirror, the heavily-polished dark brown dining table, and the numerous pieces of gleaming brassware filling every available space. On the wall was the same picture of Donald and me, taken when I must have been twelve months old, and in the dark alcove still stood that handsome, smart soldier, now sitting in his chair near the fire, contentedly filling his pipe.

I had never been allowed to go into the parlour without my grandma, so I waited until it was time to go, and as we passed the door, asked her if I could have a look inside.

'You can, Alan. I'll come in with you.' I expected this to be her answer.

Nothing had changed. The most pleasing things I saw were the shiny brass coal scuttle and the gleaming brass poker and stand.

I hadn't felt guilty for delaying this visit, and still didn't feel it was essential to make regular visits now. In those eleven years, nothing had changed. My grandparents looked the same, and the house and garden were still filled with those happy memories. But when I waved goodbye to them and happily walked down the garden path, through the gate, across our field, over the road and into the park, I didn't realise that was the last time I would ever speak to them.

Within the next year, they were forced out of their home. The council, having decided to sell our field for building land, moved them into sheltered housing. Soon after this, my grandma died.

My shame lies alongside guilt. After returning to Wigan, there had been many opportunities to go and see them, but I didn't take them. I found out, only by accident, that my grandma was ill, from someone I met in Wigan town centre, who also told me where she was being looked after. I immediately went to see her, but she didn't recognise me. I stood there, staring at her drifting in and out of sleep; she looked peaceful, but she was dying. I had never seen a person dying; that would have been bad enough, but this was my grandma, the cornerstone of my life.

At her funeral, I was distraught. I didn't cry during the service or afterwards, but during the "get together" I disappeared. Well, into the early hours, I sat crying in our field. The house had gone; only open space was left. I was desolate.

My defence is only that I had been embroiled in a slow-starting and protracted adolescence, where my selfish inclinations were the ruling factor. These were sometimes detrimental to me; in this instance, I was left permanently scarred.

About seven months later, my grandad died. If people can die of a broken heart, then he did; they had been inseparable for many years. He hadn't been able to be at her funeral. He had deteriorated to the point where he was wandering the streets, and ended up being cared for in a mental hospital where he could be supervised to make sure he didn't cause himself harm.

It was a combination of his condition and mine that prevented me from seeing him. I was talked out of it at the hospital reception, told that he wouldn't recognise me and might even say or do things to upset me. They also felt that, still grieving for my grandma, I might not be able to face up to such a visit.

I never saw my grandad again. I didn't even go to his funeral, though this at least wasn't my fault. He died shortly before I joined the RAF, but my father and brother felt I would have found it difficult to cope and decided to protect me and not tell me. It was not until two weeks into basic training that my brother sent me a telegram. I could have had a few days compassionate leave, but declined. It was all too late. I was already much stronger, both physically and mentally, and more able to handle things. The future lay where I was, on camp.

These memories of my grandparents will forever remain clear. Their lasting influence means that today my character is old-fashioned, which to me is a compliment.

If my grandparents came around the corner, I know he would say, ‘Eee, thar a rum lad,’ and she would give me a huge spoonful of malt.

# Facing the Future

# Joining Up

I arrived at the RAF Recruitment Station in a frightened and incredibly nervous state, eventually finding myself in a transition billet with about twenty other boys. The tension during those three days bordered on the unbearable. Consequently, I have only a blurred memory of much of this time, although some things remain clear. First, throughout the entire three-day period, I remained very tense and frightened. What was strange about this was that I didn't have an eczema or asthma attack. Second, our small group of hopeful recruits-to-be were moved from room to room and from building to building. The main objective was to show us a very brief overview of Royal Air Force life: the many opportunities to travel, the varied sports available and the highly-developed career structures were the most prominent areas covered, although there was a brief lecture and film sequence describing the importance of the basic discipline-training techniques.

I am not certain whether my earlier interviews had pencilled me in for a particular length of service and career choice, but the final decision was definitely made during those three days at the recruitment station. I was offered a twelve-year career in the Armament Section. Qualifications from my apprenticeship days exempted me from Parts One and Two of the RAF examinations, which were deemed necessary for an airman to progress through the ranks. Because of this, I wasn't going to be involved in mundane matters like guns, bombs and general ammunition, but would be assigned to the new defensive section: guided missile systems. I suddenly felt important. Without any hesitation, I accepted immediately, and was soon swearing an oath to abide strictly by the Official Secrets Act. At the end of those three days, my brylcreemed quiff was replaced by a severe crewcut. Then I was given a train ticket to RAF Bridgnorth which provided those essential basic discipline training techniques, i.e. square-bashing.

The fundamental objectives of this basic training were to help you to reach your top physical and mental condition. After this training and final medical, I was still eight stone seven, but now feeling super fit and much more alert; the many drill procedures, honed to perfection, had sharpened my mental faculties. These drills were encouraged and expertly developed mainly by one corporal instructor. I had never seen a person looking so clean and smart, and with so much enthusiasm in his voice. Under such influence, I didn't shirk in my efforts to reach his demanding standards. The other corporal drill instructor was Japanese, and thankfully, on duty, only occasionally; not only were his commands extremely difficult to understand, his presence on the parade ground was frightening. The sergeant was even more remote. He wasn't physically involved teaching the drill activities, his input being limited to several visits to the billet to impart "important" information. He was quite rotund and looked out of condition, and the opinion of the recruits was that a day on the parade ground would put him in hospital for a week. I saw the officer in charge twice. Once was on the first day, when I didn't yet know the difference in status between the four men. On that day, the officer was welcoming the new group into the RAF, when all my nervous attention was fixed on the Japanese corporal. The other appearance by the officer in charge was on the final drill day before the day of the Passing-out Parade. In general terms, he praised our efforts and our accomplishment in reaching the required standards in smartness and drill. Then, after wishing us well for the future in our chosen careers, he disappeared.

# Counting the Cost

I felt completely settled in this new life, but forever attempting to thwart me were gloomy and wretched reminders of my previous existence. During basic training, there were three of these. One of them came during the daily mail parade.

We would usually be in the billet, polishing brass and boots, when the order came to line up on the parade ground. 'Right dress…attention!' The next few minutes were always the same. I stood completely still in my smartest attention pose possible, shoulders and back straight, chest out, head high and eyes completely focussed ahead. If my name and number had been called, they would not even have registered. Sometimes it seemed that the entire squad but me took three paces forward to receive letters. After the mail parade was dismissed and we returned to the billet, the entire room was silent except for the rustlings of unfolding pages. I never received any letters. I fought back my mopish tendencies by working harder on my spitting and polishing. There was nothing to do about the situation – there was no one to write to from my previous life, so final had been the leaving of it. Correspondence with pub, dance, even cricket friends was a possible answer, but it wasn't the right one. Two of my grandparents' wise sayings would come to mind – 'If something is worth doing, it's worth doing well,' and, 'It's no good accepting half measures.' These two maxims helped to block out any form of communication which might keep me connected, however distantly, to my previous existence. I didn't want to be bothered with anything to do with Wigan anymore.

It was in these very early days of the mail parade that I faced up to a dangerous situation, using my grandma's trusted maxim, 'Actions speak louder than words.'

It all happened in the first fortnight of the square-bashing discipline, when I was bullied. For no apparent reason, another recruit displayed an immediate air of superiority towards me. It started from the moment he first saw me, and intensified when he realised that I never took the three paces forward to receive letters. From then on, the excitement of the day's events, discussed and evaluated over the long evenings "spit and polish", was spoiled by his taunts and jibes, all directed at me from his bed across from mine at one o'clock. I would be happily working on the evening routine, listening to the background sounds of familiar songs of the time, such as Craig Douglas singing *Only Sixteen* or Cliff Richard singing *Living Doll*; when these were on the wireless, for me, it created the perfect atmosphere. Then my gaze would land on his bed, only to see him looking at me with a sneering superiority.

He showed his self-importance by bragging to me; according to him, the dimples on his boots had already disappeared, his brass buttons, buckles and badges were gleaming, and you could cut your finger on the creases down his best blue uniform. He showed his disdain by a stream of demeaning comments: 'You should have joined the Navy, your best blue trousers look like a pair of bell-bottoms…by the time you've got rid of your dimples and polished your webbing, I'll have finished my Trade training.'

It was obvious that I was his chosen victim, probably in an attempt to achieve some level of "bragging" rights. I classified him as a bighead and tried to ignore him, but always rose to the bait and defended myself. However, the constant jibing started to irritate me, especially when he became even more cynical and sarcastic.

It came to a head during the second week of square-bashing. At some point in the evening, it was inevitable that I looked towards his bed. It was like stopping smoking; the moment you decide to stop, you want another cigarette. The moment I decided not to look at him, the more I wanted to look. Of course, when I did look, he was looking at me. He always seemed to be laughing at me.

'Can you write?' came the taunting question.

'Course I can. That's a daft question,' I replied.

Then, with his most sneering look:

'I've already got four letters from four different girls. How many have you got?' he crowed.

'Listen, when my locker gets filled with all my fan mail, I'll use yours. You won't be using it – you won't get any letters.'

He was enjoying himself.

'When we go on mail parade why don't you stay in the billet and try to catch up to me with your spit and polish? I mean to say, the stage you're up to now, I was at that stage after three sessions. Why don't you admit it? What girl wants to bother writing to somebody like that? No wonder you don't get any letters. I bet you never had – '

*Crash!*

My self-control had vanished. I picked up an empty glass bottle from the bedside locker and threw it with all of my might at him, without taking any thought or aim at all. Sometimes you need luck; I was lucky then on several counts. First, and most important, the bottle missed him. Slightly to the right of the direct line between me and him, in the centre of the room, was the large, black, coal-burning stove with its circular chimney disappearing into the roof area. The bottle smashed into the chimney, shattering into a thousand pieces. The entire billet went silent. The bully, who had been sitting on the front edge of his bed to be nearest to me when directing his taunts, went white.

'I've had enough of you. You're a big headed bully and I'm going to tell the corporal!' I shouted. It was the silence in the room that brought me to my senses. I saw the mess on the billet floor. What if the sergeant was to come through the door? It would probably be civvy street for me; throwing glass bottles at fellow recruits would be judged as definite grounds for instant discharge.

I set to work with the brush, sweeping up, collecting and disposing of all the broken glass, which had scattered over a large area. In silence, still looking shaken, he moved out of the way, to the next bed. Nobody helped me, but eventually, it was finished. This was the second piece of luck; now if the sergeant came in, with every trace of glass removed, he would be none the wiser.

Whilst on my hands and knees, I had come to another decision. After clearing up all the glass, I walked along the two lines of beds and apologised to the other recruits, shaking hands with all of them, feeling stronger with each handshake, especially when they said he deserved it and wished I'd hit him. I left the bully till last.

'I'm sorry for what I did. I'm glad that bottle didn't hit you.'

'So am I. It could have killed me.'

'Can we forget it happened? Can we shake hands and be friends?'

'I was hoping you'd ask me.'

He accepted my handshake, at the same time commenting on my inability to aim straight. 'I'm glad you're not a good shot. If we ever have to throw a grenade, I'll do it.'

Just a few minutes ago, this would have been another sneering comment, but now in this reformed situation, his words had settled pleasantly into the usual light hearted banter displayed in the billet. This was the third count in which I was lucky.

The bullying stopped, and I remained able to have a full part of life in C Block.

However, the mail parade was still upsetting. Then, one day when glancing through a recruit's newspaper sent from home, I spotted an advert for weekly football coupons. This was my answer. The form was filled in and posted, and within one week, I was taking three steps forward to at last collect a letter. This was another moment that became a blur, but once again I remember the eyes, the eyes of the smart and clean corporal. This corporal, normally in complete control, seemed to show in those blue eyes clear signs of disbelief. He never commented, but must have instantly realised that he would be forever receiving football coupons addressed to "that little imp from C Block". I secretly practised those three steps forward, which happened three times; on the final one, there seemed to be a moment of smiling understanding in the corporal's discerning eyes.

The second gloomy reminder of my previous life came when the squad was given a forty-eight hour pass at the halfway point of our basic training, when everybody seemed to be heading in the same direction, home.

I sat listening to the others discussing the weekend, looking forward to seeing their girlfriends and wives, and showing off in their "best blue".

'What about you, Alan? Where are you going?'

'Oh, I think I'll just stay here and blanco my webbing. I'll be ready for Monday morning at least.'

'You're not staying here, are you? You'll be all on your own. What if you bump into that Japanese corporal?'

'I'll just stand to attention and hope I can understand what he's saying.'

'Listen, why don't you come with me? There's plenty of room at our house, and my parents won't mind.'

This was Bob. I looked at him.

'Are you sure they won't mind?'

'No, they'll be pleased to see what kind of friends I've found.'

Gratefully, I accepted his offer. After being resigned to staying on the camp, now, instead of languishing in solitary confinement, I found myself sent to Coventry.

Bob's parents were very friendly; I was made welcome, provided with good food and my own bedroom. On the Saturday afternoon, Bob took me to the local pub, introduced me to four of his civilian friends, and disappeared. Whatever instructions he had given them to make me welcome certainly worked: I never felt like a stranger.

The Saturday night timetable wasn't strange either; it was exactly what I was used to; meeting in the pub for a few drinks then moving on to the local dance hall.

Inside, however, there was a difference. The four boys instantly joined up with a group of at least six girls – not to please me, just their normal Saturday night. I had never been part of a group before, especially one where the girls were in the majority. On that Saturday night, my "best blue" and strange accent made me the centre of attraction.

'Hello, love. Where have you sprung from?'

'Come and tell us all about yourself.'

'Oh, what's your name? Will you be coming here every week?'

I didn't feel uncomfortable; none of them quite reached the level of the mill girls. Perhaps having a few drinks and being surrounded by those songs and those happy Saturday night people, as well as being away from the scrutiny of the Japanese corporal, all helped to soften the impact of the girls' welcome.

All their greetings and comments were not dangerous, just friendly.

It was also nice to be asked to dance. This was the first time a girl had ever asked me to dance, and this happened regularly throughout the evening. We had only just joined them when it began.

'Oh, I'll have to dance with you – I've never danced with a soldier before.' My hand was taken and I was led to the dance floor.

'You're all very friendly, aren't you?'

'Oh, yes. And it's nice to see a stranger, especially a soldier.'

'I'm not a soldier, I'm an airman. I'm in the Royal Air Force. I'm staying with Bob this weekend. Do you know him?'

'Oh, yes. He's not here tonight, is he?'

'No, he's with his girlfriend.'

'Oh, well,' she said, looking disappointed. 'You sound funny when you speak. What's your name?'

'Alan. What's yours?'

'Sandra. What do you do in the RAF? Do you fly planes?'

'No.'

'What do you do, then?'

The recent memory of signing the Official Secrets Act was still clear.

'Well, it's top secret; I'm not allowed to talk about it.'

'Ooh.'

The music ended.

'Will it be OK to ask some of your friends to dance? What's her name, her in the red dress?'

'That's Jean. She'll dance with you.'

'Right, Sandra. Thanks again. I'll see you later.'

All the girls were welcoming and friendly, but despite having the last waltz with one, I left with the lads.

On the Sunday afternoon, it was out to the pub; Bob returned later after spending the weekend with his girlfriend.

Going back to the camp, my thoughts kept revolving around that Saturday night timetable – pub, drinks, dance, always the same routine. Nothing was changing.

Anyway, thanks to the hospitality and kindness of Bob and his parents, the forty-eight hour pass had gone very well, freeing me from a lonely weekend and the possibility of having to face the Japanese corporal.

The third reminder came on the final day. On that day, relatives and friends were invited to watch the march past of the final parade, led by the station band. It was not just a grand occasion; for many visitors, especially parents, it was a proud and wonderful moment. For many of the fathers, memories of their own experiences of service life, never forgotten, became more immediate and meaningful; the entire shebang could be relived.

After the show was over, allotted areas were given over to civilians, to allow them to mingle and reminisce. There were differing observations from people as to the general quality of the show, but all were united in praise of their own sons.

'You were magnificent.'

'I couldn't stop crying.'

'You look wonderful.'

'This is the proudest day of our lives.'

This was the worst reminder. I had done my bit. I too was smart and shining in my best blue and brass, but there was no one to praise me, no one to be proud of me, no family to share my moment.

Lads from the billet stopped and introduced me to their parents and relatives.

'This is Alan from C21.'

'Hello, Alan! Another smart boy! They must be proud of you.'

'This is Alan from my billet. He showed me how to get the dimples off my boots.'

'Hello, Alan! I can see my face in those boots – well done!'

The more introductions, the more upset I was becoming. I did my best to avoid them, continually moving between the parade ground and the safer confines of the billet. The walk between them was more comfortable than standing awkwardly alone in the happy crowd and less lonely than sitting in the billet. I just had to brace up to the situation, telling myself that this was a one-off day, and there wouldn't be many designated parents' and relatives' days in the future.

# Clutching at Straws

So, with basic training completed, feeling physically fit and mentally efficient, I was on my way to another camp, RAF Yatesbury, to start a sixteen-week basic Trade Training Course. It was always a question of basics in those early months, so this course was designed to cover a number of very important ones:

- Basic assembly of missile and preparation for system testing.
- Basic assembly and installation of explosive components.
- Testing procedures of explosive compounds.
- Basic repair, modification and replacement of missile launcher structure and launcher plant assembly.
- Basic electro-magnetic, electro-mechanical and hydraulic-related parts and procedures of both missile and launcher.
- Knowledge of propulsion system components.
- Knowledge of explosive components.
- Knowledge of transportation and handling equipment.

This type of working day, a mixture of intensive theory and practice-related techniques and procedures, needed a high level of concentration. My engineering background helped me to relate too much of the mechanical and hydraulic information, but I struggled, sometimes hopelessly, in the electro-magnetic field. Looking up into the body of the missile revealed nothing but a jumbled-up maze of uncoordinated and meaningless wires. Consequently, most of my spare time in the evenings was spent in trying to make sense of it all. I knew, however, that with extra persistence and by asking for help from the instructors during working hours, I would eventually see and reach the light at the end of the tunnel.

I gradually realised that keeping busy was the key to settling into RAF life. During basic discipline training, the working day had always started at early morning reveille and continued to lights out. The trade training was similar, with the working day monopolising most of the time, so I was busy and happy. There was nothing superficial or trivial about the importance of this life. I looked forward to every day; my total commitment to, and enjoyment of, RAF life kept me physically and mentally active, and my loneliness stayed hidden. But work finished at five o'clock, so then I would eagerly visit the camp gym, strictly for definition purposes and for general fitness, but also to keep up my spirits.

It was at weekends, with nearly all the billet empty, that the hidden loneliness surfaced. I tried exercise routines, showers, reading, for both work and leisure, and visiting the NAAFI to at least see people and maybe converse with somebody.

My grandma would have said I was clutching at straws; she would have been right. Nothing worked. It was a relief, in those early weeks of trade training, when Monday morning arrived, and I could once again be involved in the working atmosphere with friendly and fun-loving colleagues.

About four weeks into the course, three of the lads had an invitation for me.

'Why don't you come out with us next Saturday, Alan? It's better than stopping in here.'

'Well, thanks, Michael. I am getting a bit fed up of stopping on the camp. Where are you going?'

'It's great. We go into Chippenham, to the NAAFI club. It's always crowded, and there's loads of girls. There's a good pub near there and we have a game of darts and a few drinks. It's great.'

'Will the others not mind me coming with you?'

'No, it was Archie suggested that you came with us.'

Michael's idea of a great night out sounded familiar. I accepted their invitation, though, and decided that wherever they wanted to go, I would go too, and do whatever they wanted to do; that was how desperate I'd become. As it turned out, their Saturday night out was very similar to what I had been used to before, which was the one I was longing to leave behind, the only difference being that there was no band. The timetable now was the pub and then dancing to records in the NAAFI club in Chippenham.

The club catered for servicemen, providing them with a place to meet for various socials and entertainments, with dancing on Saturday nights. At the end of the evening, I would probably still be faced with the question – what to do? Spend time with a girl, or go back to the billet? But now I was thinking: should I change the pattern and go further than my previous experience had taken me?

The pattern which had established itself had never altered. I loved to be in a girl's company, to walk out of the dance hall with her, escort her to the bus stop and arrange to meet on the Sunday for an afternoon walk and evening pictures. Apart from those twelve weeks with one girl, I never felt an inclination to form a lasting relationship. This didn't worry me at all. I was quite content, knowing that there always seemed to be a girl available to dance with and to walk to the bus stop.

So, what to do at the end of the first night at the NAFFI club? Not surprisingly, I went back to the camp and the safety of the billet. The next few weeks were no different; I danced with girls all night, but always shied away from any further involvement. These weeks were the unhappiest of my life, because I suddenly felt trapped.

I had tried my very best, yet four months after walking away from that wretched second life, I still hadn't managed to escape from its clutches. I didn't know what I was searching for, but felt that there must be a solution to my unhappiness. However, the loneliness, which had begun from the moment I was carried screaming away from my grandparents, and continued through school days, work and these early days in the RAF, was now strengthening and taking a deeper hold on me.

It seemed there was worse to come. Christmas was looming, and this was troubling me. Would I be spending Christmas alone in the billet? Grappling with the problems of what to do and where to go always left me feeling beaten, completely isolated, with no one to raise my crushed spirit. Grandma would have said that I was right at the end of my tether. She would have added, when I had made my decision of what to do, that I had chosen the lesser of two evils. There were several gloomy weekends to face before Christmas. Should I remain in the billet, literally suffering in silence, or go out, to the pub, darts, NAAFI club and girls? It was only a slow fuse, delaying the inevitable, whatever that might be, but I chose to go out. I had to cling on somehow and hope for a miracle.

# The Miracle

So, once again I set off on my Saturday night out. It was by now early December; it would soon be Christmas and nothing had changed. I went into the dance hall and took up my usual position on the fringe of the crowded floor, trying to look relaxed and carefree, but feeling, of course, dark and gloomy. To the sound of *Some Enchanted Evening,* I searched the room for a dancing partner,

"Who can explain it, who can tell you why?"

Then my heart seemed to stop, before reacting violently. I was drawn across the room. Each step caused greater chaos.

'May I have this dance?' My voice sounded distant and strange.

She didn't speak, but smiled and held my hand. Then we were dancing, or more accurately, I was holding on tightly to her with the words "Once you have found her, never let her go" pounding in my head. This was the moment. I had no control.

The impact was immediate and unstoppable.

That night I couldn't sleep.

I had asked to see her again the following Saturday. Then I had waited.

Please, please, say yes…

'I have to work next Saturday night; I start at eight o'clock.'

'Can I see you in the afternoon, then? We can go for a walk. When it's time for you to start work, I can go back to camp.' I don't know how I had managed to speak those words or how they sounded.

'Are you not coming here next week?'

'No. I don't want to if you're not. What if I see you at twelve, then we'll have time for a long walk?' My heart was beating fast, my head was pounding and I was floundering. I had never felt like this before. I had asked her three times; I couldn't keep asking her.

'All right. That'll be good.'

I hadn't been able to speak. Holding her hand tightly had felt wonderful.

I couldn't sleep. Incredibly, I still didn't know her name. Being afraid of saying the wrong thing, I hadn't asked her in case she took offence. Why I thought she might have done, I don't know.

Saturday finally arrived. I was waiting in front of the NAAFI club very early.

Would I see her again? Relief surged through me as I saw her in the distance.

'Hello. I hope you haven't been waiting long.' She had the softest, most gentle voice I'd ever heard.

'No, but I didn't want to be late. I'm glad you've turned up.'

She held my hand and we just started walking. Things began to become clear. Here was the answer to my questions, in fact, the answer to everything. I couldn't take my eyes away from her. She was lovely: a slim figure, short, light brown hair, naturally wavy in an old-fashioned style, a fresh complexion and beautiful blue eyes. I found out during this first walk that I towered over her by a massive two and a quarter inches.

The longer we walked, the more unsettled I was becoming. I couldn't help it, but I had to face it. I needed to know.

By mid-afternoon, our wanderings had taken us into a small park.

'Let's sit down here for a few minutes. I'd like to ask you something. It's nice and peaceful here, isn't it?'

'Yes, it's lovely. Everything looks good,' she said happily. Already I liked to hear the way she said 'good', in her gentle Scottish accent. But now I had to make myself speak.

'Will you be working next Saturday?'

'No, I work every other weekend, why?'

'Can I see you next week, then?' I had stopped breathing. Don't say no; I don't think I can ask you again.

'If you want to.'

*If you want to!* I repeated these words to myself. This was one of the most wonderful moments of my life.

'I do. When we have to leave each other today, I'll hardly be able to wait for next Saturday. Do you think we can meet early and spend all day together?'

'If you like.'

*If you like!*

'Well, if I meet you at nine o'clock, is that OK?'

'Yes, that's all right.'

I had never been so happy. My tense, agitated, scared and lonely self had vanished. It was a miracle. I felt as if I could jump to the moon.

'This is the best moment of my life. Everything looks good.' I'd pronounced it *guid*, showing off, trying my best to be Scottish. She was still holding my hand, but was now looking at me in a strangely serious way. I stopped being Scottish.

'If I tell you my name,' I said, 'will you tell me yours?' At last!

'I might,' she said teasingly.

'Well, my name's Alan.'

'That's a nice name. It's calm and peaceful. I'll like to call you Alan.'

'Tell me your name then.'

'Elizabeth.'

'Oh, I like that name. It's old-fashioned. I'm old-fashioned too. What if I call you "my Elizabethan"? I could write a letter to my Elizabethan.'

She let go of my hand and turned away from me. It was several seconds before I realised she was crying. I immediately began to panic. What had I done wrong? What could I do now?

'Elizabeth, what's wrong? I'm sorry. Why are you crying?'

Sitting in a secluded corner of that empty park, listening to her painful sobbing, not knowing the reason and not knowing what I should do, was definitely the worst moment of my life.

Eventually, she took my hand again and rested her head on my shoulder. This was reassuring, but I was still lost.

After a while she spoke. 'I'm sorry, Alan. It's not your fault. I promise I'll tell you why I was crying, but please, not today. Will you just call me Elizabeth, even when you write to me?'

*Even when you write to me!* I kept repeating her words to myself. I could hardly believe it. Even when you write to me.

'You mean you'll let me write to you?'

'Yes, we could write to each other.'

'I'm going to write to you every night. Sometimes we won't be able to see each other for a while, but when I'm posted to a permanent camp, I'll find a way of seeing you on your free weekends.' My thoughts, and my words, seemed to be running together. I no longer needed to hold my breath, or to pray.

'Elizabeth, thanks to you, everything is good.'

'Except for one thing.'

'What do you mean?'

'I'll have to teach you how to say *guid*, even if it takes a lifetime.'

She was now smiling and cheerful. When we held hands and started walking again, I felt as if we were dancing. We were already sweethearts. It was wonderful.

Holding hands with Elizabeth, I was taken to a special place. For the first time in my life, I was in a sunlit room. Printed on the inner circle of her wedding ring is the meaning of my name – Harmony. From that very first Saturday afternoon, this is how and where we lived.

# Synopsis

I start my "first life" standing by the side of my mother's coffin. My father is absent on war duties. In this semi-abandoned state, I am placed in the care of my grandparents.

I have many happy memories of this life, between the ages of four and eight, feeling safe, protected and loved, my character allowed to develop with an innocent freedom. My experiences are daredevil, frightening and sad; I face bullies with knives and big fists, suffer a near drowning, get myself stuck high in the sky and even hide from a murderer.

I fail in one test of self-discipline, where I literally can't take my medicine, throwing my grandparents' concern, worry and love down the kitchen sink. This incident, minor in retrospect, is one of my saddest memories.

My big brother Donald, always four years older, makes several appearances. He is an extension of the care and protection provided by my grandparents, and is there to help me through various difficulties. At the start of my "second life", when I am suddenly thrust into an inexplicably dire situation, he is there to hold my hand.

This second life, from 8 to 21, sees Donald's disappearance and my having to rely entirely on myself. My father is demobbed, and quickly decides to remarry, and I am taken away from my grandparents and prevented from seeing them. Sinking, rather than settling, into a deplorable existence, I face 13 years of continual rejection, isolation and loneliness, which test to the limit the sound principles instilled during my early years.

Although forbidden to see my grandparents, I find a way to stay in touch and am able to secretly "visit" them. This helps to give me the spirit and determination to keep out of trouble and maintain decent moral standards.

I am able to cope outwardly with my parents' demands, but inwardly, I lose ground fast. Lacking in confidence and increasingly anxious, I try various ways of escape, including drink, religion and sport, all ending in failure.

Finally, as my grandparents, full of wise and wonderful words, would have said, 'Alan is right at the end of his tether.'

This is the moment when I escape for ever from my second life.